Mandolin Exercises

FOR DUMMIES®

A Wiley Brand

Mandolin Exercises

FOR DUMMIES®
A Wiley Brand

by Don Julin

FOR DUMMIES®
A Wiley Brand

Mandolin Exercises For Dummies®

Published by
John Wiley & Sons, Ltd.,
The Atrium, Southern Gate,
Chichester,
www.wiley.com

This edition first published 2013

© 2014 John Wiley & Sons, Ltd, Chichester, West Sussex.

Registered office

John Wiley & Sons Ltd, The Atrium, Southern Gate, Chichester, West Sussex, PO19 8SQ, United Kingdom

For details of our global editorial offices, for customer services and for information about how to apply for permission to reuse the copyright material in this book please see our website at www.wiley.com.

The right of the author to be identified as the author of this work has been asserted in accordance with the Copyright, Designs and Patents Act 1988.

For general information on our other products and services, please contact our Customer Care Department within the U.S. at 877-762-2974, outside the U.S. at (001) 317-572-3993, or fax 317-572-4002.

For technical support, please visit www.wiley.com/techsupport.

A catalogue record for this book is available from the British Library.

ISBN 978-1-118-76953-9 (pbk), ISBN 978-1-118-76949-2 (ebk), ISBN 978-1-118-76952-2 (ebk)

10 9 8 7 6 5 4 3 2 1

Contents at a Glance

Table of Contents

Introduction

*I*f you're anything like me, playing mandolin is one of your favorite things to do in the world, and on a good day you even sound pretty good at it. But do you ever dream about being a much better mandolin player? If so, the time is right to stop dreaming and start working. These pages contain exercises and concepts that I've collected from 30-plus years of mandolin playing, and I'm happy to share them with you. *Mandolin Exercises For Dummies* contains loads of exercises for your fingers as well as for the musical part of your brain, involving some simple music theory concepts along with an understanding of where things are located on the mandolin fingerboard. One of the primary challenges for you as an evolving musician is the physical aspect of playing your instrument. Mandolin players' hands need to be comfortable with a very specific set of activities or fine motor skills. The physical exercises in this book range from warm-up routines including stretching and relaxation exercises, to scale and arpeggio workouts. Each of the exercises requires specific skills for both hands, including (deep breath) alternate picking, tremolo, slides, hammer-ons, major scales, three types of minor scales, pentatonic scales, moveable scale and arpeggio patterns, double stops, chromatic fingerings, three-string chord forms, rhythm patterns, and plenty of other things to get your hands in shape.

Your brain gets a bit of a workout too, because many of the exercises require you to apply each scale pattern or sequence to different chords or keys. Don't worry if you aren't up to speed on all 12 major and minor keys yet . . . you soon will be. By working with this book, you gain the necessary understanding of major scales, three types of minor scales, major, minor, seventh, diminished, and augmented chords, as well as arpeggios, diatonic harmony, and a bit of good-old greasy blues. I even include a chapter on applying your scale and arpeggio knowledge to the fascinating world of improvisation.

About This Book

Feel free to thumb through this entire book, stopping to work on any section that you're interested in. You don't need to work through this book from cover to cover or in any particular order. Think of it as your long-term companion: you can explore new chapters and return to familiar ones for years to come. Each chapter is self-contained, and if any specific skills are called for, I cross-reference them. Many basic mandolin skills used in these exercises are contained in *Mandolin For Dummies,* and so if you want to know more, pick up a copy of that book as well.

Most of the exercises I present here aren't genre specific – they're general mandolin skills that you see in a variety of musical styles. I don't include any esoteric exercises that only apply to classical mandolin technique.

I'm well aware that people don't learn the same things in the same way, and so I explain many of the concepts in a variety of ways. On the printed page you see neck diagrams, standard music notation, tablature, chord diagrams, left-hand fingerings, suggested pick direction, and rhythm patterns. In addition, I include over 150 examples from *Mandolin Exercises For Dummies* in audio form so that you can hear them before trying to read them. Download the audio at `www.dummies.com/go/mandolinexercises`.

Here are some tips for getting the most out of this book:

- **Listen to the downloadable audio tracks!** Listen to the audio tracks! Listen to the audio tracks! Listen to the audio tracks! Oh, and did I mention, listen to the audio tracks! Music is sound, and unless you're already a great sight-reader, you gain much more of an idea of what each exercise is supposed to sound like from the audio tracks than from looking at the page. An added bonus is that some of the audio tracks are designed so that you can play along with the rhythm section, allowing you to step into the spotlight as the soloist.

- **Get comfortable with your metronome.** Play many of the exercises in this book very slowly at first, making sure to get every note perfectly clear and focusing on individual finger strength. When you achieve a pleasing clear sound, slowly increase the tempo, changing the focus from strength to co-ordination. Your metronome is the best way to ensure that you're playing steadily. The tendency for everyone is to play the easy parts fast and harder parts more slowly. Your metronome keeps you honest. Think of it as a speedometer in your car: without it you may be going much faster or even much slower that you think, resulting in a penalty or worse. Sometime the truth hurts a little and the metronome certainly tells you the truth.

- **Repetition is the key.** Imagine going to the gym and spending only 30 seconds on each piece of exercise equipment before moving on to the next one. You continue this process for 40 minutes and then take a shower and go home. That's not the best use of your 40 minutes at the gym. The same applies to mandolin practice. Find an exercise or a chapter that interests you and stick with it for 30–40 minutes per day for multiple days. Over the course of a few days or weeks, you start to see a transformation in your strength and co-ordination, allowing you to play tunes or licks that were simply impossible before.

Foolish Assumptions

I make the following assumptions about you:

- That you have a mandolin. If not, it may help!

- That you have a basic understanding of the mandolin and can already play a few tunes. You should also have a good handle on holding and tuning the mandolin, strumming chords using rhythm patterns, alternate picking, and simple tremolo. If you aren't sure about some of these skills, get yourself a copy of *Mandolin For Dummies* and do some revision.

- That you have a copy of *Mandolin For Dummies* and have worked through some of the tunes and exercises.

- That you enjoy a variety of music genres and are open to the mandolin being used in many styles of music.

- That you have indeed downloaded the audio tracks at www.dummies.com/go/mandolinexercises. If not, stop everything and download them now!

Icons Used in This Book

You can find the following icons in the left-hand margins throughout this book.

This icon offers helpful little tidbits of information that can make your practice easier and more productive.

I use this icon to indicate important points that are worth bearing in mind.

I include this icon when I feel the need to explain something that's interesting but not essential. You can safely skip these paragraphs if you prefer, because the text doesn't make any difference to how you perform the exercise. These items tend to be more theoretical in nature. Music nerds love these parts.

To draw your attention to a common mistake to avoid, I place this icon beside the relevant text to give you a heads-up.

This icon tells you to listen to the track in which I demonstrate a technique or tune. These tracks are invaluable when you're practicing a specific skill.

Beyond the Book

Before you do anything else, I suggest that you go to www.dummies.com/go/mandolinexercises and download the audio tracks. Don't try to use this book without them. After you download the audio tracks, you're ready to begin.

Why not also check out the book's online cheat sheet at www.dummies.com/cheatsheet/mandolinexercises - containing loads of quick, handy hints and tips to help you get the most from the exercises in this book.

Where To Go from Here

Mandolin Exercises For Dummies is intended to be a resource that improves your mandolin playing. The timeless exercises presented in this book are general in nature and should be memorized and played in every key, using every possible fingering, everywhere on the neck, at all tempos, with expression! Or as close to that as you care to get.

Exercises are great but knowing a tune and playing it with a good technique is better. Learn tunes you like. It doesn't matter if you like Irish fiddle tunes, Monroe style bluegrass tunes, blues, jazz, choro, or classical music. Pick music you enjoy and that you will stick with. It's also really important to play with other folks. Find a jam session, bluegrass festival, mandolin orchestra, singer songwriter that like the sound of the mandolin, a church group, or any situation that has you playing mandolin with other people. This will ensure that your mandolin playing goes much further and beyond the point of finishing this book.

Learn to play by ear! All of your mandolin heroes learned to play by ear, imitating sounds they heard on the radio or on early recordings. Play along with your favorite recordings. If the mandolin parts are just too fast, you can easily find low cost software or even an inexpensive app that will change the speed of a recording without changing the pitch. I like The Amazing SlowDowner http://www.ronimusic.com/.

Make your own back-up tracks. The tracks that come with *Mandolin Exercises For Dummies* were created on iReal b http://irealpro.com/., an app for an iphone and Band-in-Box http://www.pgmusic.com/ which is traditional software available for mac or pc. Back-up tracks are more fun than playing with a metronome. More fun equals more time you will want to spend playing your mandolin.

Above all, play your mandolin and have fun!

Part I

Getting Ready to Practice

getting started
with

**Mandolin
Exercises**

In this part . . .

- ✔ Mentally prepare yourself to play the mandolin.
- ✔ Warm yourself up with stretching, coordination and strength building exercises.
- ✔ Refresh your memory of left and right hand mandolin basics.
- ✔ Review your knowledge of reading tablature, chord and neck diagrams.

Chapter 1

Getting the Basics Sorted: Mandolin Fundamentals

In This Chapter

▶ Checking out right-hand fundamentals

▶ Using your left hand effectively

▶ Following written music

You can't play the mandolin without using your hands and fingers. So in this chapter I run through the left- and right-hand basics (check out *Mandolin For Dummies* for more details). I take the opportunity to cover the following: holding the pick, basic picking techniques, left-hand fingerings, and proper left-hand grip. I also include reading tablature, chord diagrams, and neck diagrams.

If you already know some of this material, taking a second look never hurts. Reminding yourself is usually good, unless of course it's a reminder about how awful it feels to trip over and put your foot through your favorite mandolin!

Tuning Up

Before you can make beautiful music on your mandolin, you need to be in tune. Listen to Track 1 of the downloadable audio tracks (www.dummies.com/go/mandolinexercises) and tune to me if you like to tune by ear, or use your favorite tuning method. For further information on a variety of tuning methods be sure to have a flick through *Mandolin For Dummies*.

Covering a Few Right-Hand Basics

One of the most important elements in mandolin playing is having a strong, co-ordinated, and organized right hand. This hand is responsible for rhythm, tone, dynamics, and speed. It needs to stay relaxed and loose while you're playing. Small adjustments in the way you hold the pick can dramatically change your tone or even your ability to play at faster tempos. (I give you tips on speeding up in Chapter 16.)

Another often-overlooked part of mandolin playing is maintaining proper pick direction. Many of the exercises in this book include elements that deal with pick direction to help strengthen and develop your left and right hands.

Holding the pick

Beginners often pass over this basic skill, but sooner or later you need to come to grips with the way you hold your pick:

1. **Make your right hand a loose fist with your thumb sticking up a bit.**

2. **Lay the pick on the side of your first finger, as shown in Figure 1-1 (a).**

3. **Place your thumb over the pick so that you're holding the pick between the pad of your thumb and the side of your index finger (b).**

4. **Hold the pick as loosely as you can.**

   A death grip may be great for subduing aggressive Klingons, but it's no good for playing the mandolin. Too tight a grip on your pick guarantees bad tone and uneven tremolo, and may even get you thinking that you'll never be able to play quickly.

5. **Position your right hand so that the pick hits the strings somewhere near the end of the fingerboard. (This is often called the 'Sweet Spot'.)**

Some players support their right hand by lightly touching the bridge with the heel of the right hand. Some don't touch the bridge but support their right hand by dragging their third and fourth fingers on the top of the mandolin or the pick guard (which is sometimes called the finger rest). Some believe that you shouldn't touch the top of the mandolin at all. What all players can agree on, however, is to support the mandolin by resting your arm on the rib as shown in Figure 1-1 (c).

For more details of picks, holding the pick, and methods of support for the right hand, see Chapter 5 of *Mandolin For Dummies.*

Figure 1-1:
Holding the
pick.

Getting up to speed with alternate picking

If you had to pick one technique that defines mandolin playing it would be alternate picking. *Alternate picking* in its simplest form is just a series of pick strokes following an even down-up, down-up pattern. Mastering this technique is essential to playing certain popular mandolin styles such as fiddle tunes, rags, bluegrass, swing, choro, Bach, and any music that has a steady, even flow of notes.

Tremolo is a well known mandolin technique based on alternate picking. Owing to the lack of sustain when playing a mandolin, mandolin players over the years have developed the *tremolo,* which is basically rapid alternate picking to imitate the continuous sustained sound of the violin bow.

See the following exercise for a basic set of alternate-picking drills. Many of the scale and arpeggio exercises I present in this book (see the chapters in Parts II and III, respectively) require a decent understanding of alternate picking. You can consider the following figure (which I demonstrate on Track 2) to be a test. If you're prepared to work through the exercises in this book, you can perform these four types of alternate picking: (a) eighth notes (quavers), (b) eighth-note triplets, (c) sixteenth notes (semiquavers), and (d) sixteenth-note triplets.

If you're struggling a bit with these alternate-picking drills, visit Chapter 5 of *Mandolin For Dummies,* where I describe alternate picking and tremolo in more detail.

Track 2

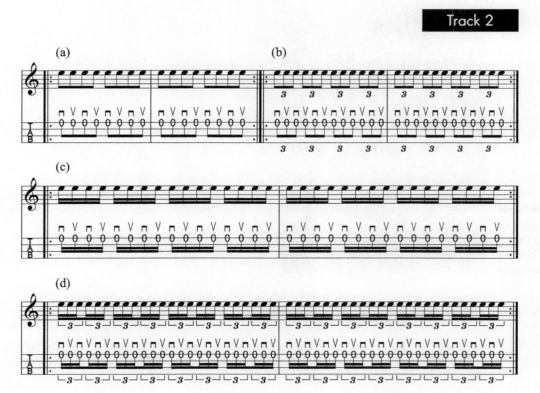

Letting Your Left Hand Do the Talking

The left hand is responsible for making the actual note pitches, as well as ornaments including different types of slurs that connect notes together smoothly. Position shifts (playing in different regions up and down the neck) require a good understanding of a variety of left-hand fingerings.

Clarity and sustain require clean fretting of each and every note, which can happen only when you understand proper left-hand technique. If you aren't 100 per cent confident with your left-hand skills, take a look at Chapter 6 of *Mandolin For Dummies.*

I describe some useful finger warm-up exercises and techniques for you in Chapter 2.

Using a proper grip

Here are a few pointers for getting the most out of your left hand:

✔ Support the neck with your thumb and keep some space between the palm of your hand and the back of the neck, as shown in the following **Figure 1-2.**

✔ Try to keep your wrist fairly straight. Avoid any sharp angles by pushing your wrist up or down (see the two photographs).

✔ Angle your fingers so that they point back at your midsection (see the upper photo).

Don't try to keep your fingers parallel to the frets; that's a guitar technique and doesn't work well for the mandolin.

✔ Bend the last knuckle in each finger so that you fret the strings with the tip of your finger (see the lower photo).

Figure 1-2:
Using a
proper grip.

Figuring out fingerings

The following figure is a diagram of a mandolin fingerboard including the names of the notes. Notice that the sharps and flats are designated by black dots in a similar way to how sharps and flats on a piano are black keys.

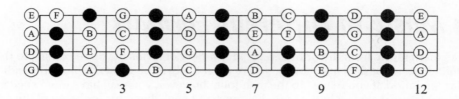

Mandolin left-hand fingerings are much more like those of the violin than of a guitar, in that each finger is responsible for two frets. With guitar, the basic rule is one finger per fret. By looking at the following figure, you can see that for the mandolin you need to play the fifth fret with your third finger.

If your mandolin teacher suggests that you play the fifth fret with your fourth finger, you're taking mandolin lessons from a guitar player and should look for another teacher. See the following figure for basic open (or first) position fingerings.

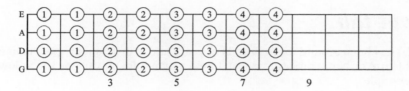

When playing up the neck, the fingering concept remains two frets per finger. I demonstrate all scales and arpeggios in this book in moveable closed positions and open position. You may hear other mandolin players talk about 'positions' when playing up the neck. If players refer to, say, 'third position', they mean playing up the neck, and so your first finger would be at the fifth or sixth fret, which is usually played by the third finger, hence the term 'third position'.

The best way to make your fingering and positioning second nature is to practice scales day and night, driving your neighbors crazy. Check out Chapter 3 for major scales, Chapter 4 for (the no-less-important) minor scales, Chapter 5 for pentatonic and chromatic scales (great for improvising), and Chapter 6 for how to expand scales to more than one octave. For arpeggio practice, flip to Chapter 7 for major ones, Chapter 8 for minor ones, Chapters 9 and 10 for sevenths, and Chapter 11 for diminished and augmented ones. Don't worry if any of these terms are new to you; I explain everything thoroughly in each relevant chapter.

Throwing in left-hand ornaments

Beyond just playing the notes, the left hand is also capable of adding some personality to your melody with left-hand ornaments. Rather than being knick-knacks for your mantelpiece, these ornaments include slides, hammer-ons, pull-offs, mutes, and so on. I discuss performing these techniques and recognizing what they look like in printed music in detail in Chapter 6 of *Mandolin For Dummies.* (How did you ever manage without it!)

Reading Music in Different Formats

You can learn music from the printed page in a variety of forms. If you're coming to the mandolin from a classical instrument, you're most likely to be comfortable with reading standard notation. If you're new to the mandolin, however, you may have more success reading tablature. I also include chord diagrams and neck diagrams for many of the exercises in this book, which are basically illustrations of the fingerboard with indications of where the notes are. Any or all of these methods are useful when learning to play an instrument.

Whatever method you choose, be sure to listen to recordings of the song, lick, or exercise you're trying to master. Music is sound, and printed music is merely a way to archive and communicate music from person to person or even generation to generation. Nobody gets out sheet music and starts reading it because they like the way it makes them feel. Be sure to download all the audio demonstration tracks for this book from www.dummies.com/go/mandolinexercises.

Trying out tab

Tablature (tab) has been around for hundreds of years and is instrument-specific, meaning that guitar tablature or banjo tablature doesn't help a mandolin player. See the following figure for an example.

The four horizontal lines represent the four pairs of strings on the mandolin. The numbers refer to fret numbers, and so a '7' placed on the first or highest line indicates a note at the fifth fret of the e-string. By the way, the name of this note is B.

As an additional aid to the exercises in this book, I place pick-direction markings, fingerings, and note names above the tablature. Not all exercises contain all the additional markings, but I include them wherever possible to make sure that you understand the proper way to perform the exercise.

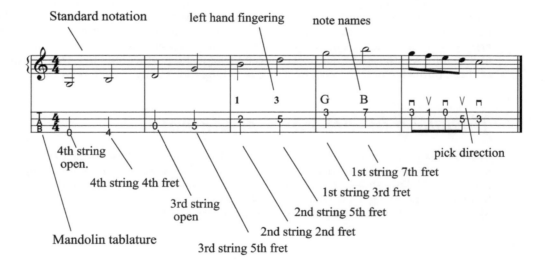

Understanding chord diagrams

Chord diagrams are basically a vertical illustration of a certain region of the mandolin fingerboard. The dots indicate where to put your fingers to make a specific chord.

A circle placed directly above a string where the headstock of the mandolin would be indicates an open string, whereas an 'x' in that same location tells you not to play that string. Numbers along the bottom of the chord diagram indicate which fingers to use on each string. See the following figure for an example of a chord diagram.

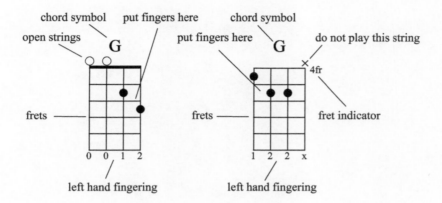

Part IV is where it all comes together: Chapter 12 brings arpeggios and scales together with some diatonic arpeggio exercises, Chapter 13 for a serious rhythm workout using three-string chords, and Chapter 14 gives you a look at some improvised solos in different musical styles and even gives you a chance to do a bit of improvising yourself.

Interpreting neck diagrams

Neck diagrams are similar to chord diagrams but are presented horizontally instead of vertically. Neck diagrams typically show more frets that chord diagrams do and are used more often for scales (see the chapters in Part II) and arpeggios (flip to the chapters in Part III).

The numbers inside the dots or circles are finger numbers; the numbers below the illustration are fret numbers. The following figure is an example of a neck diagram.

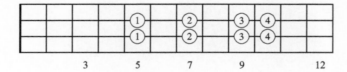

Chapter 2

Limbering up to Get into the Groove

In This Chapter

▶ Relaxing mind and stretching body

▶ Thinking about posture

▶ Warming up your fingers

Playing the mandolin can be quite an athletic activity, requiring strength, endurance, and co-ordination in both hands. And yet, music is more of a mental or creative art requiring concentration and focus, which can happen only when your mind is relaxed. This chapter offers you a few ways to limber up your fingers, hands, and arms with easy exercises, stretches, and drills. I also present suggestions for correct posture. But because playing an instrument isn't only about the physical, I give some quick relaxation tips too. Some of the following suggestions and techniques may seem a little new-agey or like something you see at a meditation retreat, but with so many people leading stressful lives, with careers and family obligations, everyone can benefit from some basic relaxation.

Stretching Your Fingers and Relaxing Your Mind

Quite possibly you play the mandolin to help escape from the stresses of life. Therefore you want to be as relaxed as possible while playing; plus, without doubt you play better and get much more satisfaction when you're properly prepared to play.

The aim of these exercises is to bring about connection of your mind and body. Sit in a straight-backed chair with both feet evenly on the ground. Position your sitting bones/pelvis evenly in the seat of the chair. Take a deep breath and hold it for a few seconds. Slowly exhale, relaxing your arms from your fingertips all the way up your arms, through your shoulders and neck, releasing any tension. Repeat this deep breathing exercise a few times.

Closing and opening your hands

If you've been trying to play the mandolin with your elbows, think again and try using your fingers instead! This exercise starts the blood circulating in your hands, fingers and arms:

1. **Place your arms at your side, with both arms hanging free extending toward the floor, close both hands into fists, hold for a few seconds, and then open your hands, spreading your fingers apart.**

2. **Repeat this procedure, but this time with your arms extended out to the side.**

3. **Repeat once more with your arms extended overhead all the way, so that your elbow locks straight; feel those different muscles and tendons stretching.**

Flexing your fingers

I divide the finger exercises in this section into three basic groups: flexibility, co-ordination, and strength.

Your fingers have many small muscles and tendons that need to be flexible and strong to play the mandolin, so you need to do a little preventive maintenance for your fingers. Your hands and fingers need to be in top physical condition. Proper stretching can prevent injuries.

Stretching

Flexibility is crucial to great mandolin performances:

1. **Hold your left arm upright, bent at the elbow, so that your fingers are in front of your face.**

2. **Place the tips of your left-hand fingers into the palm of your right hand.**

3. **Push your right hand gently against your left-hand fingers, extending them back. When you can feel the stretch, hold it for a few seconds before releasing.**

4. **Switch the procedure around to stretch right-hand fingers by placing them into your left palm and repeating the stretching exercise.**

Don't push too hard, because you can pull a muscle or tendon.

Co-ordination

Playing the mandolin requires a good amount of co-ordination with your fingers. Here are a few finger-co-ordination exercises.

Exercise 1:

1. Start with your left hand in a relaxed position and touch the tip of your first finger to the tip of your thumb, followed by your second finger to your thumb.

2. Cycle through this exercise touching all four of your fingertips to your thumb tip.

Do this exercise with both hands, increasing speed as you get comfortable with it.

Exercise 2:

1. Lay your hand palm down on a table.

2. Try lifting each finger, one at a time, while making sure that the other fingers stay on the table.

3. Repeat this exercise with the other hand.

Most people find that the ring finger is the hardest one to isolate.

Exercise 3:

1. Lay your hand on a table, palm up.

2. Lift each finger, one at a time, while making sure that the other fingers stay flat on the table.

3. Cycle through this exercise a few times using all four fingers.

4. Repeat the exercise with the other hand.

Strength

After you're stretched out and your co-ordination is getting better, look at a simple strength-building exercise that many guitar and mandolin players use.

Simply squeeze a rubber ball many times with each hand. Doing so increases strength, but remember that overall stretching and co-ordination are more important than sheer strength.

Extending your arms

Here are two good stretching exercises that loosen you all the way up your arms, through your neck, and even reach your neck.

Exercise 1:

1. Sit in a straight-backed chair, positioning yourself at its front edge.

2. With your right hand, grab the front right leg of the chair. Now straighten your back and turn your head to the left as far as you can. You should feel the stretch all the way into your neck.

3. Repeat the exercise with your left hand on the left front leg of the chair, turning your head to the right as far as you can.

Exercise 2:

1. Stand up straight with your shoulders perpendicular or at a 90 degree angle to a wall, at arm's length from it.

2. Place the palm of your left hand against the wall, with fingers pointing toward the ceiling.

3. Extend your arm, locking your elbow, so that it's fairly straight, and then turn your head to the right. You should feel the stretching from your wrist to your neck.

4. Repeat using your opposite hand.

Quietening your mind

You can do finger- and arm-stretching exercises all day long and yet still hear the voice of your nagging boss, disgruntled customer, or co-worker echoing around in your head and preventing you from relaxing enough to enjoy playing your mandolin. Mental relaxation is as important as physical limbering up.

In this exercise you take a moment to examine each of your five senses, trying not to pass judgment, good or bad. The object is to be present in this moment and not be distracted by things in your past or to worry about things that haven't happened. Here's how it goes:

1. **Look around you and really notice simple objects or colors in the room.**

2. **Take a deep breath and try to identify any smells – maybe the smell of bacon that you cooked for breakfast or the scent of flowers blooming outside your window.**

3. **Listen carefully and try to identify all the sounds around you – maybe the washing machine running, the traffic outside, the sound of a songbird in a tree, or even the sound of your own breath as you inhale and exhale.**

4. **Focus on taste by running your tongue along your teeth; is that bacon from breakfast still lingering?**

5. **Notice physical sensations, perhaps the feel of the chair on your back, your feet on the floor, or any aches and pains.**

By doing this exercise with all five of your senses without passing judgment, you lower the noise and clutter that everyone has in their heads: by focusing on the right here, right now, you eliminate thoughts that can interfere with enjoying your time with your mandolin. I think you'll find this relaxation exercise useful. Of course, it isn't specific to mandolin players.

Positioning Yourself Properly

Correct posture makes practicing and playing your mandolin much easier and prevents possible injuries. Many mandolin players perform music while standing, but the vast majority of practice happens while sitting. I cover proper posture for sitting and standing with the mandolin in detail in *Mandolin For Dummies*.

Here are some things to keep in mind when practicing the mandolin:

- ✔ Sit in a straight-backed chair if available; try to avoid the overstuffed sofa.
- ✔ Lean forward slightly; avoid leaning back.
- ✔ Place both feet on the floor approximately shoulder width apart; some people can play the mandolin with one leg crossed over the other.
- ✔ Try to keep your shoulders level.
- ✔ Relax from your neck all the way down to your fingertips.

Observe yourself in a mirror. If you look relaxed, you most likely are relaxed; otherwise, you're most likely not relaxed and you need a little adjustment.

Warming Up Your Fingers to Play

Most musicians agree that you play better when you're warmed up and feeling loose. All athletes warm up, and maybe musicians should as well. One approach is to play some tunes you're working on until you feel sufficiently warmed up.

Fiddle tunes work very well for warming up, because they are fairly easy to play and both left and right hand skills are needed in order to play them properly. You may already know 'The Arkansas Traveler', 'The Girl I Left Behind Me', or 'The Drunken Landlady' which can all be found in *Mandolin For Dummies*. If you choose that approach, play through a few fiddle tunes three or four times slowly, making sure that you fret each note clearly and perform each pick stroke correctly before playing very fast or very loudly.

Simply running warm tap water over your hands for a few minutes will also work to warm them up. I once saw a young Chris Thile in a public men's room just prior to his performance running warm tap water over his hands. Maybe that's his secret weapon?

Heating things up: Right-hand warm-ups

As a mandolin player, your right hand is responsible for timing, tone, and dynamics. The single most important right-hand motion used in playing the mandolin is repetitive alternate picking, which is simply the motion of down-up-down-up and so on. In this section I provide right-hand warm-ups that fall into two groups: *tremolo,* which is rapid alternate picking while remaining on one note or a slowly moving melody, creating a sustained effect; and skipping from string to string while maintaining proper alternate picking. Both exercises are incredibly useful.

Tremolo

Tremolo may well be the definitive technique on the mandolin. The rapid back and forth picking creates the illusion of sustain, similar to the bowing of a violin.

The following warm up exercises use measured tremolo, meaning that each stroke is in time with the beat of the music. Think of this process as working out at the gym, where you perform a certain number of repetitions of each specific exercise before moving on to the next part of your routine.

Play the following warm-up exercises very slowly at first, gradually increasing speed, making sure to remain relaxed. Keep a very loose grip on the pick and keep the tremolo very even.

I demonstrate. Listen to Track 3 of the downloadable audio tracks at `www.dummies.com/go/mandolinexercises` for this warm up tremolo exercise.

Track 3

Make the warm-up and co-ordination exercises in this chapter part of your regular routine for many years. At first, go through them as warm-up exercises, trying to get each note as clear as possible while using the correct pick direction and proper left-hand fingering. After a few months, try increasing speed while maintaining clarity. As the speed increases, these exercises become more about co-ordination than simply warming up.

String-skipping warm-ups

The following warm-up exercises are co-ordination exercises that sound a bit like classical piano studies and are designed to train your right hand to keep moving in an alternating down-up motion while moving from one string to another. This exercise is a variation on a set of right hand exercises made popular by the American mandolin player/teacher John Moore, who just so happened to be a young Chris Thile's mandolin teacher.

Playing these exercises slowly and accurately is very important. You may find this very difficult at first, but just like any other co-ordination based activity, (like juggling) if you spend a little time on it you will be able to do it. I suggest setting your metronome to 80 beats per minutes (bpm) or maybe even slower, matching the metronome with down-strokes on the click, and with the up-strokes landing between the clicks. Over time, increase the speed but make sure to keep each note clean and clear. Playing this faster than you should but a little bit sloppily doesn't help! When you're comfortable at speeds above 120 bpm, try cutting your metronome to half note or two clicks per measure. You can read more about metronome practice techniques in Chapter 16.

Listen to Track 4 for a demonstration of how to warm up your right hand using some string-skipping exercises.

Track 4

Discovering left-hand warm-ups

Your left hand is responsible for the correct note or *pitch* but also plays a large part in how clear the notes sound. By building strength and dexterity in your left-hand fingers, you notice that the notes sound clearer and even louder. The following warm-up exercises are designed to limber up and strengthen your left-hand fingers. For more left-hand technique tips, check out Chapter 6 in *Mandolin For Dummies*.

Individual fingers

This exercise helps to develop independence with each of your left-hand fingers (but not so much that they want to leave and join the other hand!).

This exercise isn't difficult, but don't be fooled: the object is to play it very slowly and try to get the clearest notes with the most sustain possible. Be sure to follow the left-hand finger numbers located directly above the tablature and play it using the consecutive down/up pattern.

Tetrachords (partial scales)

These warm-up exercises focus on tetrachords played on one string.

Tetrachord is just a fancy term for four-note patterns that make up half a scale. You find these patterns in all the major, minor, and blues scales used for exercises throughout this book, and so getting your left-hand fingers familiar with these patterns has major benefits as you work through the exercises. Another value in using tetrachords as a warm-up is that each one uses all four left-hand fingers equally and therefore gets the blood flowing in all four fingers.

I divide the tetrachords in this section into three groups: (a) tetrachords found primarily in major and natural minor scales; (b) tetrachords containing chromatic passages of three frets in a row; and (c) tetrachords with a minor third (or three-fret gap) as seen in the harmonic minor scale.

A good practice strategy is to focus on one group of tetrachords per day, playing all group (a), (b), or (c) (check out the following figure). When you have group (a) tetrachords sounding clear on the d-string, transfer the same patterns over to the g-, a-, and e-strings. Notice that even though the pattern is the same, each string feels different and requires some practice to get a clear, buzz-free tone. The next day, pick a different tetrachord group and work that group through all four pairs of strings.

Listen to these tetrachords on Track 5.

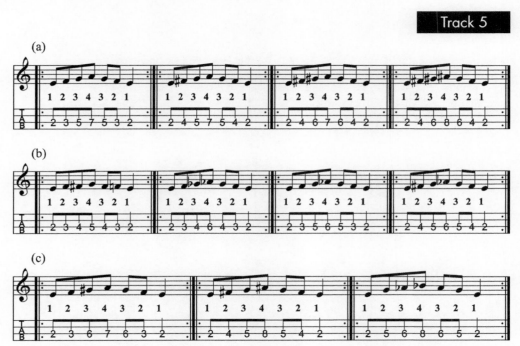

Part II
Learning Scales

In this part . . .

✔ Learn, practise and master a variety of scales.

✔ Get familiar with major scales, minor scales, pentatonic and chromatic scales in moveable closed patterns, first position, and on one string.

Chapter 3

Mastering Major Scales

In This Chapter

▶ Playing major scales using four moveable patterns

▶ Locating major scales in open position

▶ Practicing major scales on one string

*I*n this chapter I introduce you to major scales. No, that's not a character from *The Phil Silvers Show* (perhaps you're thinking of Colonel Chord). In fact, major scales are the cornerstone of all Western music. The sound is so common that almost everyone can recognize it from a mere suggestion of the phrase do-re-mi-fa-so-la-ti-do (think Julie Andrews if it helps).

The scale comprises a series of *intervals* (or a distance) between notes of a *whole step* (a distance of two frets on your mandolin) or a *half step* (the distance of one fret). The interval series for the major scale goes as follows: whole step, whole step, half step, whole step, whole step, whole step, half step. Starting on any note, this pattern results in the highly recognizable major scale.

In this chapter you discover how to play major scales in four closed position moveable patterns, were one fingering pattern can be simply moved up, down, or even across the neck to play the scale in a variety of keys, in the ever useful open position, and on one string.

Discovering Four Moveable Major Scale Patterns

Each major scale has a unique number of sharp or flat notes. For example, in the key of G major, you play all the F notes as F sharp (F♯). Therefore, people say that G major has one sharp. In the key of E flat (E♭), you flat all the E, B, and A notes, and so you use E♭, B♭, and A♭ instead.

No major scales contain sharps *and* flats, always just one or the other.

Each piece of music indicates the number of sharps or flats (commonly called *the key*) at the beginning. But bear in mind that the key can also change in the middle of a piece, so keep your eye open for the key signature.

The following figure shows three different key signatures: (a) C major, (b) G major, and (c) E♭ major. The sharps and flats written in the key signature are on the line or space of the affected notes. For example, in the key of G major the sharp sign is on the line that represents the F note, therefore making all F notes into F♯ notes. Notice that the key of C major has no sharps or flats.

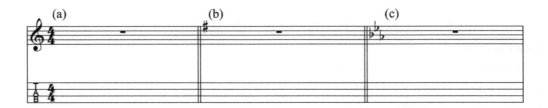

Scales aren't only an important element in melody – everyone's favorite part – they're also responsible for harmony: things such as *counterpoint* (two melodies that sound good together), chords, embellishments to existing melodies, and the complete creation or improvisation of a solo. All these elements of a piece of music have a relationship with one or more scales. When you're proficient at scale and scale patterns in a variety of keys and positions, you're ready to learn to play a wide variety of music.

Moveable (or closed) major scales are organized into four patterns for each scale. The pattern names are based on which finger of your left hand plays the first or *root* note. These patterns are sometimes referred to as FFcP or four finger closed position patterns.

The four moveable patterns I describe in this section contain no open strings, and each pattern for any scale needs to sound exactly the same. For example, pattern 1 for the G major scale sounds just like pattern 2, 3, or 4 of the G major scale: different fingering, but the same sound. Memorizing these patterns not only allows you to play in any key, but also makes it possible to play in any key anywhere on the neck of the mandolin.

Always use your metronome when practicing scales. Start each of the sequences at a slow tempo of 60 beats per minute (bpm) and gradually work your way up to higher speeds. Playing slowly allows you to hear each note and tell whether you're fretting each note clearly or creating a buzzing sound.

Don't advance to faster tempos until *all* the notes are clear.

Major scale pattern 1

Major scale pattern 1 starts with your first finger on the *root note* (the note that is the name of the scale) and finishes with your fourth finger on the *octave* (or higher root note). This pattern uses two strings on the mandolin. You can play it anywhere on the neck, depending on which major scale you're practicing.

The following figure shows the E major scale as a neck diagram, standard sheet music, and tablature (tab). To play this pattern, place your first finger on the E note, which is on the second fret of the d-string, and follow the neck diagram and tab. Make sure you use the suggested fingerings. You can listen to this scale on Track 6 at www.dummies.com/go/mandolinexercises.

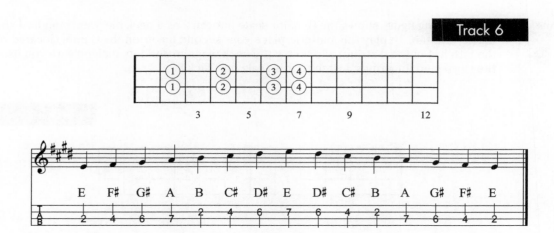

 Now try practicing the pattern 1 G major scale by moving this pattern up three frets. Remember that this is the very same pattern 1 you played in the key of E but by placing it three frets higher on the same strings you are playing pattern 1 major scale but this time in a different key. Place your first finger on the G note located at the fifth fret of the d-string. When you can play this major scale pattern in the new position, practice the scale sequence demonstrated in the following figure and on Track 7. This sequence uses 16th notes (semi-quavers) played with alternate picking (which I describe in Chapter 1). When you've mastered this sequence, work on playing it in all 12 keys by simply placing your first finger on the root note of your choice and performing the major scale pattern 1 sequence.

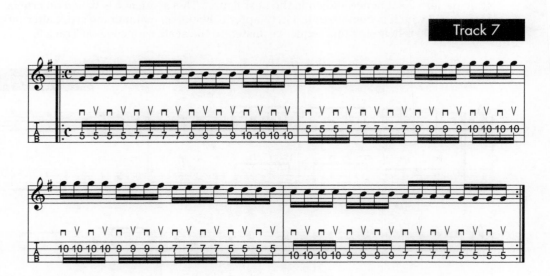

Major scale pattern 2

Major scale pattern 2 starts with your second finger on the root note of the scale and finishes with your first finger on the octave. This pattern uses three strings on the mandolin. You can perform it anywhere on the neck, depending on which scale you're running through.

 The G major scale shown in pattern 1 needs to sound the same as the G major scale shown in pattern 2: same sound, different fingering.

The following figure shows the G major scale pattern 2 as a neck diagram, standard sheet music, and tab. To play this pattern, place your second finger on the G note (located on the fifth fret of the d-string) and follow the neck diagram and tab, making sure you use the suggested fingerings. Listen to this scale on Track 8.

Track 8

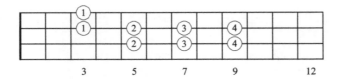

Now try the pattern 2 F major scale by moving this pattern down two frets. Place your second finger on the F note located at the third fret of the d-string and play the major scale pattern 2 sequence shown in the next figure . This sequence is based on crucial scale sequence 2 which is demonstrated in Chapter 6. Focus on maintaining strict alternate picking while rehearsing this sequence. Listen to the scale sequence on Track 9.

Track 9

Try the preceding scale sequence using major scale pattern 2 in all 12 keys by simply placing your second finger on the root note of your choice and playing this major scale pattern 2 sequence.

Major scale pattern 3

Major scale pattern 3 starts with your third finger on the root note of the scale and finishes with your second finger on the octave. This pattern uses three strings on the mandolin. You can play it anywhere on the neck, depending on which scale you're getting to grips with.

The following figure shows the pattern 3 A major scale as a neck diagram, standard sheet music, and tab. To play this pattern, place your third finger on the A note, which is located on the seventh fret of the d-string. Listen to this scale on Track 10.

Track 10

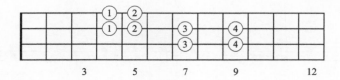

You can shift the pattern 3 A major scale to the key of D major by moving it over one string (lower) so that the first note becomes the seventh fret of the g-string. The following figure shows the sequence for the D major scale, using alternate picking. This sequence uses crucial scale sequence 3 which is demonstrated in Chapter 6. Pay close attention to pick direction when crossing from one string to another. Listen to this scale sequence on Track 11.

Track 11

Try the preceding scale sequence using major scale pattern 3 in all 12 keys by simply placing your third finger on the root note of your choice and playing this major scale pattern 3 sequence.

Major scale pattern 4

Major scale pattern 4 starts with your fourth finger on the root note of the scale and finishes with your third finger on the octave. This pattern uses three strings on the mandolin. You can play it anywhere on the neck, depending on which scale you're licking into shape.

The following figure and Track 12 demonstrate the D major scale pattern 4 as a neck diagram, standard sheet music, and tab. To play this pattern, start by placing your fourth finger on the D note (located on the seventh fret of the g-string).

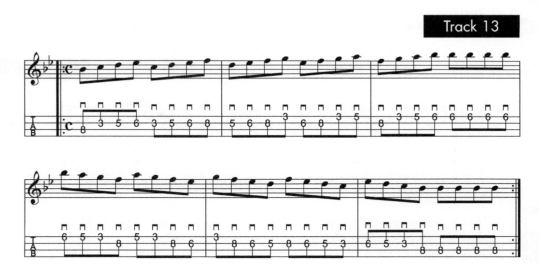

I show the D major scale in two ways in this chapter. Make sure that D-major scale pattern 3 sounds the same as D major scale pattern 4: same sound, different fingering.

Now try your hand at practicing the B♭ major scale by moving this pattern to the eighth fret of the d-string. This sequence is based on crucial scale sequence 4 which is demonstrated in Chapter 6. Play this sequence using down-strokes only. Check out the following figure and Track 13.

Try the preceding scale sequence using major scale pattern 4 in all 12 keys by simply placing your fourth finger on the root note of your choice and playing this major scale pattern 4 sequence.

The following figure shows a simple major scale sequence in the key of G major using major scale pattern 1. Memorize this sequence. Try playing this sequence in other keys by moving the major scale pattern up or down a few frets or even over to the adjacent string keeping in mind that the root note or the name of the scale will be played with your first finger and the octave will be played by your fourth finger.

In this exercise I give you an opportunity to test your knowledge of the mandolin fingerboard. Follow the chord progression shown in the following figure by playing the appropriate major scale to match the chords, using the sequence from the previous figure. Play the G scale for the G chord, the B♭ scale for the B♭ chord, and so on. Be sure to listen to Track 14 to see how this exercise works. If you need help finding some of the root notes on the mandolin fingerboard see the fingerboard diagram in Chapter 1.

Track 14

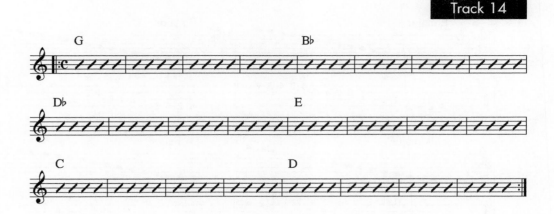

I like to keep you busy, and so when you can get through these six keys with the practice track using pattern 1, try memorizing the same sequence using patterns 2, 3, and 4 (from earlier in this section 'Discovering Four Moveable Major Scale Patterns'). Then go through the exercise focusing on one pattern at a time until you can complete the entire exercise using each of the four moveable major scale patterns.

When you can get through this exercise using the four moveable patterns without mistakes, try using only open-position major scales and even one-string major scales. Good luck!

Studying the First Seven Frets: Major Scales in Open Position

Mandolin players tend to like to play in *open position* (also called *first position*), which means playing in the first seven frets of the neck and using open strings whenever possible. Open position is also the most comfortable place on the neck to play scales and melodies, because of the spacing of the frets. (See how close to each other they become as you move further up the neck.)

The following figure shows all the available notes in each of the 12 major scales while staying in open position. Notice that these scales extend beyond one octave and also include partial scale segments that extend higher or lower, covering the entire range of open position. The root notes of each scale are indicated by a + placed directly above the tab.

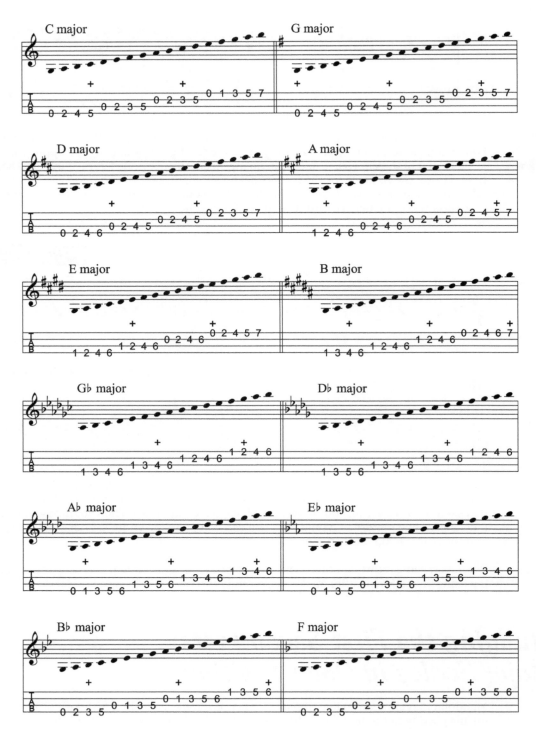

When you're comfortable with these open-position scale patterns, you can work on incorporating some of the scale sequences used throughout this book. Just memorize the sequence and apply it to the open-position patterns.

Exploring Major Scales on One String

One of the best ways to discover the upper ranges of the fingerboard is to practice playing scales on one string. Remember to pay close attention to the fingerings, shifting where indicated. Upon examination, you will find that the major scale is simply two tetrachords (see Chapter 2) separated by a whole step or two frets.

The following figure shows the one-string pattern for the E major scale, which starts on the second fret of the d-string. This pattern is also moveable by simply placing your first finger on any note and following the pattern up one string.

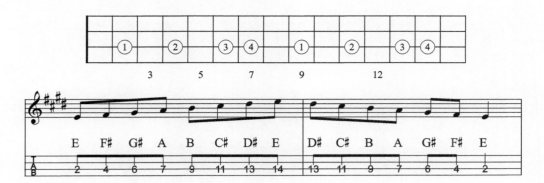

 Whenever you're practicing any of the sequences or exercises in this book, repetition is key. Think of it like going to the gym to work out: doing one or two pushups doesn't get you into shape, but 30 or 40 repetitions per day over a series of days certainly make a difference. So start working on your musical six-pack today!

Chapter 4

Discovering Three Types of Minor Scales

*T*he eternal battle of good and evil has inspired countless books, films, song lyrics, and fairy tales. In music, the contrast is often depicted with major scales (representing good) and minor scales (representing the dark side), allowing the musician or composer to tell a complex and rich story. Although less common than their major counterparts (which I describe in Chapter 3), minor scales tell tales of mystery, sadness, and loss, and they can sound haunting or even scary. So if your musical tendencies lean towards the gothic, minor scales may well fit the gloomy bill!

Unlike major ones, the minor scales that I demonstrate in this chapter come in three varieties: natural, harmonic, and melodic. All three exhibit a dark, mournful sound that's characterised by a flatted third degree of the scale, which is simply lowering the third step of the major scale by a half step (or one fret). I provide four patterns for each variety as well as open positions and scales on one string.

In addition to the flatted third, pay close attention to the sixth and seventh degrees of the scales, because these notes are the ones you alter to give each minor scale its own unique sound.

Playing Moveable Natural Minor Scale Patterns

You can arrive at a natural minor scale by starting out with a major scale and lowering the third, sixth, and seventh degrees of the scale by one half step (one fret). *Moveable* (or closed) minor scales are organized in similar patterns to their major scale cousins, in that four patterns exist for each scale (check out Chapter 3). The names of the patterns are based on which finger of your left hand plays the first note.

The four moveable patterns in this section contain no open strings, and all four patterns for any scale need to sound exactly the same. For example, pattern 1 for the G natural minor scale sounds just like pattern 2, 3, or 4 of the G natural minor scale: different fingering but the same sound.

Each natural minor scale is closely related to a major scale and even contains exactly the same notes as its relative major scale. A bit of investigation reveals that the sixth degree of any major scale becomes the root note of a natural minor scale, while it uses the very same notes as in a major scale. This concept is called the *relative minor*. If you're fairly comfortable with the major scales, getting the hang of the natural minor scales by this method is pretty painless.

The following figure shows the relative minor relationship of G major and E minor, including two octaves of a G major scale. The bracketed area that covers the notes E to E in the G major scale turns out to be the E natural minor scale. I refer to this relationship as the relative minor, because the same notes make up the scales G major and E natural minor.

 TIP Always use your metronome (see Chapter 16) when practicing scales. Start each of the exercises at a slow tempo of 60 beats per minute (bpm) and gradually work your way up. Playing slowly allows you to hear each note and tell whether you're fretting each note clearly or getting a buzzing sound. It's best not to advance to faster tempos until *all* the notes are clear.

Natural minor scale pattern 1

Natural minor scale pattern 1 starts with your first finger on the *root note* (that with the name of the scale) and finishes with your fourth finger on the *octave* (the higher root note). This pattern uses two strings on the mandolin. You can play it anywhere on the neck, depending on which minor scale you're practicing.

 PLAY THIS! The following figure shows the E natural minor scale pattern 1 as a neck diagram, standard sheet music, and tablature (tab). To play this pattern, place your first finger on the E note, which is on the second fret of the d-string, and follow the neck diagram and tab. Make sure you use the suggested fingerings. You can hear the E natural minor scale on Track 15 at www.dummies.com/go/mandolinexercises.

 TIP Listen to the audio tracks before you try to play any of the exercises in this book, and always practice with a metronome (see Chapter 16).

Track 15

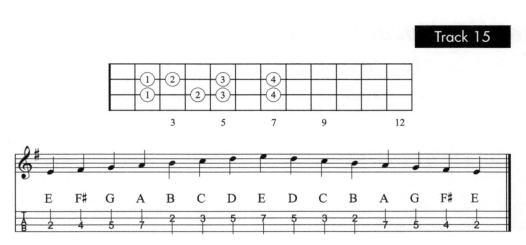

Now try your hand at practicing the G natural minor scale by moving the E natural minor scale pattern 1 up three frets, placing your first finger on the G note at the fifth fret of the d-string. Remember that this is the very same pattern 1 you played in the key of E minor but by placing it three frets higher on the same strings you are playing pattern 1 natural minor scale but this time in a different key. When you can play this natural minor scale pattern 1 in both E minor and G minor, try practicing the scale sequence shown in the following figure, which I demonstrate in G minor. This sequence uses triplets while maintaining *alternate picking,* meaning that you need to play the first set of triplets down-up-down and the next set up-down-up. Listen to Track 16 for a demonstration.

When you've mastered this sequence, try playing it in all 12 keys by simply placing your first finger on the root note of your choice and playing the natural minor scale pattern 1 sequence.

Always follow the suggested pick direction when working through these exercises. Doing so gives both your hands a great workout – like a finger gym!

Natural minor scale pattern 2

Natural minor scale pattern 2 starts with your second finger on the root note of the scale and finishes with your first finger on the octave. This pattern uses three strings on the mandolin. You can play it anywhere on the neck, depending on which scale you're practicing.

The G natural minor scale in pattern 2 needs to sound the same as the G natural minor scale in pattern 1: same sound, different fingering.

The following figure shows the G natural minor scale pattern 2 as a neck diagram, standard sheet music, and tab. Start by placing your second finger on the G note, which is on the fifth fret of the d-string, and follow the neck diagram and tab, making sure you use the suggested fingerings. To hear this played, listen to Track 17.

Track 17

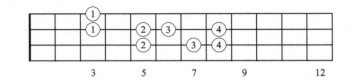

Now try the F natural minor scale pattern 2 by moving this pattern down by two frets (see the following figure). Place your second finger on the F note at the third fret of the d-string and play the natural minor scale pattern 2.

The following sequence is based on crucial scale sequence 2 (see Chapter 6). Try to maintain strict alternate picking while practicing this pattern. Track 18 gives a demonstration.

Track 18

Try the scale sequence in all 12 keys by simply placing your second finger on the root note of your choice and playing this natural minor pattern 2 sequence.

Natural minor scale pattern 3

Natural minor scale pattern 3 starts with your third finger on the root note of the scale and finishes with your second finger on the octave. This pattern uses three strings on the mandolin. You can play it anywhere on the neck, depending on which scale you're practicing.

The following figure shows the A natural minor scale pattern 3 as a neck diagram, standard sheet music, and tab. You start by placing your third finger on the A note, which is on the seventh fret of the d-string. For a demonstration, listen to Track 19.

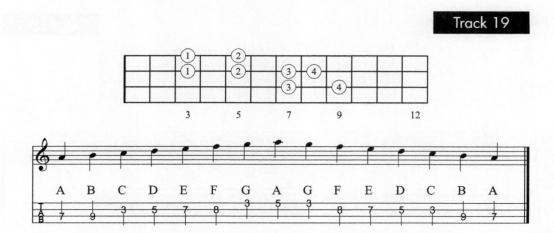

 You can play this pattern in the key of D natural minor by moving it over by one string (lower) so that the first note is now the seventh fret of the g-string. Don't you just love the symmetry of the mandolin! I show the sequence, which uses triplets, in the following figure for the D natural minor scale; you can hear it played on Track 20. This time the right-hand pattern is down-up-down for each triplet, which is commonly known as jig picking and is used in Irish jigs.

 Try the scale sequence in all 12 keys by simply placing your third finger on the root note of your choice and playing this natural minor pattern 3 sequence.

Natural minor scale pattern 4

Natural minor scale pattern 4 starts with your fourth finger on the root note of the scale and finishes with your third finger on the octave. This pattern uses three strings on the mandolin. You can play it anywhere on the neck, depending on which scale you're practicing.

 The following figure shows the D natural minor scale pattern 4 as a neck diagram, standard sheet music, and tab. To play this pattern, place your fourth finger on the D note, which is on the seventh fret of the g-string. You can hear a demonstration on Track 21.

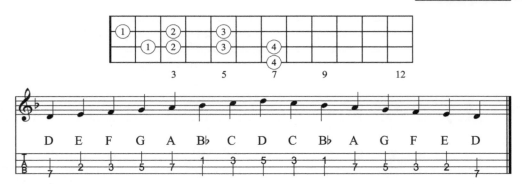

D E F G A B♭ C D C B♭ A G F E D

I show the D natural minor scale in two ways in this section. Make sure that the D natural minor scale pattern 4 sounds the same as the D natural minor scale pattern 3: same sound, different fingering.

Now try your hand at practicing the B♭ natural minor scale by moving this pattern to the eighth fret of the d-string. Play the sequence using down-strokes only. This sequence is shown in the following figure and played on Track 22.

The following figure shows a simple natural minor scale sequence in the key of G minor using natural minor scale pattern 1. Memorize this sequence. Try playing this sequence in other keys by moving the major scale pattern up or down a few frets or even over to the adjacent string keeping in mind that the root note or the name of the scale will be played with your first finger. You can hear me play this sequence in the following exercise.

You can practice the previous scale sequence in all 12 keys by simply placing your fourth finger on the root note of your choice and playing this natural minor pattern 4 sequence.

Okay, now it's time to test your knowledge of the fingerboard with this natural minor scale exercise.

Follow the chord progression shown in the following figure and play the appropriate natural minor scale to match the chords, using the sequence from the previous figure once you have it memorized. Play the G natural minor scale for the G minor chord, the Bb natural minor scale for the Bb minor chord, and so on. Be sure to listen to Track 23 to see how this exercise works. I demonstrate this exercise the first time through, you are on your own the second time.

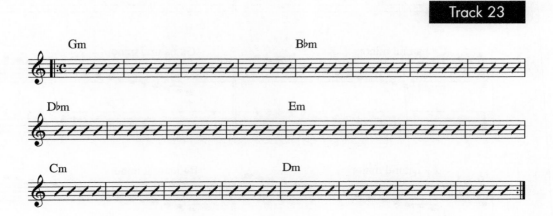

Once you can get through these six keys with the practice track using pattern 1, go back and memorize the same sequence using patterns 2, 3, and 4.

Next go through the exercise focusing on one pattern at a time until you can get through the entire exercise using each of the four moveable minor scale patterns.

Once you can get through this exercise using the four moveable natural minor patterns without mistakes, try using only open position natural minor scales and even one-string natural minor scales. Good luck!

Keeping an open mind: Natural minor scales in open position

Mandolin players tend to like to play in *open position*, which means playing in the first seven frets of the neck and using open strings whenever possible. Even though the notes of a mandolin are the same as those of a violin, and violin players of certain styles tend to avoid open strings, the open strings of a mandolin are one of the characteristics that define the mandolin sound, so don't avoid them.

Open position is also the most comfortable place on the mandolin's neck to play because of the spacing of the frets. Notice how close the frets are to each other as you go farther up the neck.

The following figure shows all the available notes in each of the 12 natural minor scales while staying in first or open position. Notice that these scales extend beyond one octave and also include partial scale segments that extend higher or lower, covering the entire range of first position. I indicate the root notes of each scale with a + placed directly above the tab.

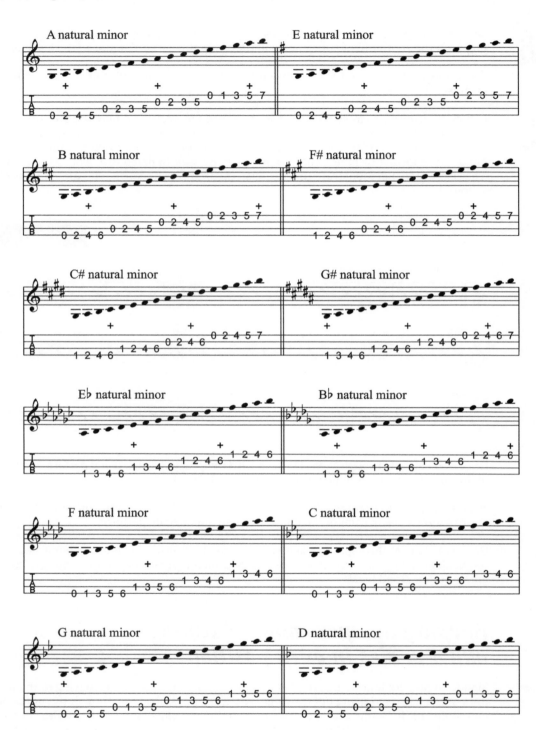

When you're comfortable with these open-scale positions, try incorporating some of the scale sequences I describe throughout this book, by memorizing the sequence and applying it to the open position scale patterns.

Figuring out the fingerboard: Natural minor scales on one string

One of the best ways to learn the upper ranges of the fingerboard is to play scales on one string. Pay close attention to the fingerings, shifting where indicated. The following figure shows the one-string pattern for the E natural minor, which starts on the second fret of the d-string. These patterns are also moveable, by simply placing your first finger on any note and following the pattern up one string. Notice that the natural minor scale is made up of two tetrachords, (see Chapter 2) separated by a *whole step* or two frets.

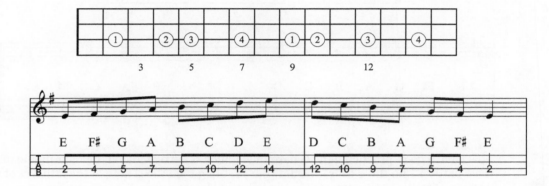

Creating Drama: Moveable Harmonic Minor Scale Patterns

The harmonic minor scale is the same as the natural minor scale (which I describe in the earlier section 'Playing Moveable Natural Minor Scale Patterns') except that the seventh degree of the scale is raised one half step (one fret). You can also start with a major scale and lower the third and sixth steps by one half step. This alteration leaves a gap of three frets between the sixth and seventh steps of the scale.

Harmonic minor scales have a mysterious sound and can conjure up images of romantic gypsy musicians, mist-shrouded castles, or eastern European folk music.

Harmonic minor scale pattern 1

Harmonic minor scale pattern 1 starts with your first finger on the root note of the scale and finishes with your fourth finger on the octave. This pattern uses two strings on the mandolin. You can play it anywhere on the neck, depending on which minor key you're practicing.

In harmonic minor scales, the distance between the sixth and seventh step of the scale is a minor third or three frets. Notice that in pattern 1, the large gap falls between the second and third fingers.

The following figure shows the E harmonic minor scale pattern 1 as a neck diagram, standard sheet music, and tab. To play this pattern, place your first finger on the E note, which is on the second fret of the d-string, and follow the neck diagram, tab, and suggested fingerings. Listen to Track 24 to hear how this pattern sounds.

Track 24

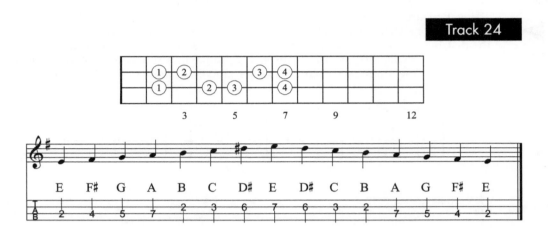

Now have a go at practicing the G harmonic minor scale by moving the E harmonic minor scale pattern 1 up three frets, placing your first finger on the G note at the fifth fret of the d-string. Play the scale sequence in the following figure using all down-strokes, as demonstrated on Track 25.

Track 25

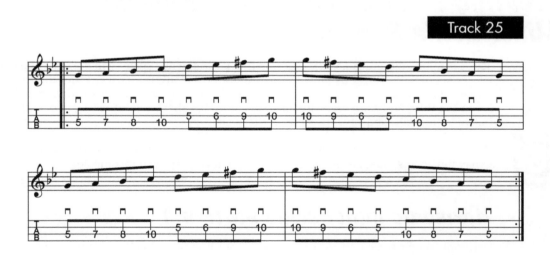

When you've mastered this sequence, try playing it in all 12 keys, simply by placing your first finger on the root note of your choice and playing the harmonic minor scale pattern 1.

Harmonic minor scale pattern 2

Natural minor scale pattern 2 starts with your second finger on the root note of the scale and finishes with your first finger on the octave. This pattern uses three strings on the mandolin. You can play it anywhere on the neck, depending on which minor key you're practicing.

You play the three-fret gap between the sixth and seventh steps of the scale with the third and fourth fingers. Extending your fourth finger that far can be a bit tricky at first, so take it slowly and remember to stretch and warm up before playing anything that requires big stretches.

The following figure shows the G harmonic minor scale pattern 2 as a neck diagram, standard sheet music, and tab. To play this pattern, start by placing your second finger on the G note, which is on the fifth fret of the d-string, and follow the neck diagram and tab using the suggested fingerings. Jump to Track 26 to hear this pattern.

Track 26

The G harmonic minor scale in pattern 2 sounds the same as the G harmonic minor scale in pattern 1: same sound, different fingering.

Now try the F harmonic minor scale by moving the G harmonic minor scale pattern down by two frets, placing your second finger on the F note at the third fret of the d-string and playing harmonic minor pattern 2.

The following scale sequence uses tremolo at the speed of six strokes per quarter note (crotchet). All mandolin players benefit from regular tremolo practice. Listen to Track 27 to see whether you can hear a tremolo speed of six strokes per quarter note.

Try playing this exercise using three down-strokes per quarter note (crotchet) at first. When you're comfortable with the down-strokes, add the up-strokes but keep your right hand moving at the same speed. If done correctly, you end up with a smooth six stroke per quarter note tremolo.

Track 27

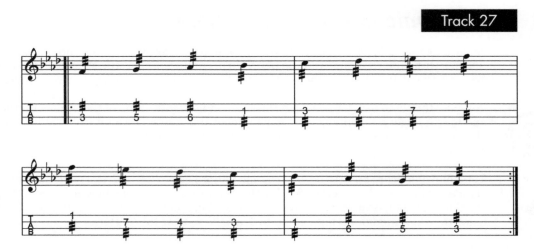

Try the following scale sequence in all 12 keys by simply placing your second finger on the root note of your choice and playing the harmonic minor pattern 2 sequence.

Harmonic minor scale pattern 3

Harmonic minor scale pattern 3 starts with your third finger on the root note of the scale and finishes with your second finger on the octave. This pattern uses three strings on the mandolin. You can play it anywhere on the neck, depending on which scale you're practicing.

The following figure shows the A harmonic minor scale pattern 3 as a neck diagram, standard sheet music, and tab. To play this pattern, place your third finger on the A note, which is on the seventh fret of the d-string. To hear this pattern played, go to Track 28.

The large gap between the sixth and seventh steps of this pattern doesn't require a large stretch, because the sixth step is on the a-string and the seventh step is on the e-string.

Track 28

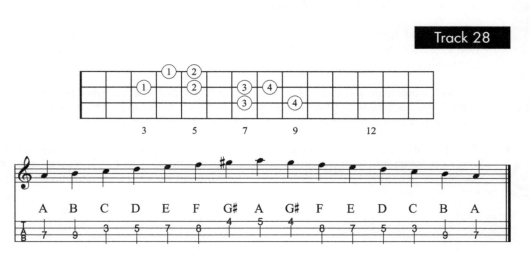

You can transpose the A harmonic minor scale pattern to the key of D harmonic minor (see the following figure) by moving it over by one string (lower) so that the first note of harmonic minor scale pattern 3 is now the seventh fret of the g-string. Remember to maintain proper alternate picking when practicing this sequence. This sequence is based on crucial scale sequence 3 which is covered in Chapter 6. Listen to Track 29 before you try to play this pattern.

Track 29

Try the following scale sequence in all 12 keys by simply placing your third finger on the root note of your choice and playing this harmonic minor pattern 3 sequence.

Harmonic minor scale pattern 4

Harmonic minor scale pattern 4 starts with your fourth finger on the root note of the scale and finishes with your third finger on the octave. This pattern uses three strings on the mandolin. You can play it anywhere on the neck, depending on which scale you're practicing.

The following figure shows the D harmonic minor scale pattern 4 as a neck diagram, standard sheet music, and tab. Track 30 provides a demo. To play this pattern, start by placing your fourth finger on the D note, which is on the seventh fret of the g-string. Notice that you end up playing the large gap in this scale with your first and second fingers.

The D harmonic minor scale pattern 4 needs to sound the same as the D harmonic minor scale pattern 3: same sound, different fingering.

Track 30

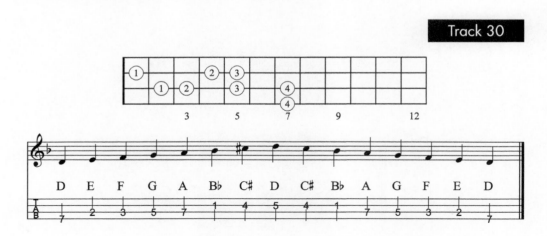

Now try your hand at the B♭ harmonic minor scale (see the following figure) by moving the previous pattern to the eighth fret of the d-string. Practice this sequence using alternate picking; the pick direction marks are directly above the tab. For help, listen to Track 31.

Track 31

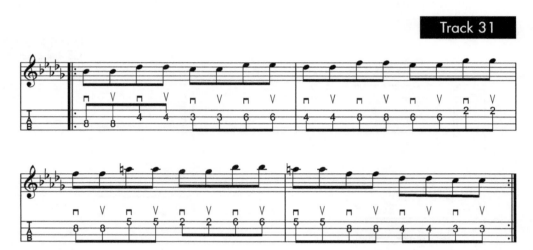

Have a go at practicing the scale sequence in all 12 keys, by simply placing your fourth finger on the root note of your choice and playing the harmonic minor pattern 4.

The following figure shows a simple harmonic minor scale sequence in the key of G minor using harmonic minor scale pattern 1. Memorize this sequence. Try playing this sequence in other keys by moving the major scale pattern up or down a few frets or even over to the adjacent string keeping in mind that the root note or the name of the scale will be played with your first finger. You can hear this simple scale sequence in the following exercise.

Okay, now it's time to test your knowledge of the mandolin fingerboard with this harmonic minor scale exercise.

Follow the chord progression shown in the following figure by playing the appropriate harmonic minor scale to match the chords, using the sequence from the previous figure. Play the A harmonic minor scale for the A minor chord, the C harmonic minor scale for the C minor chord, and so on. Be sure to listen to Track 32 to see how this exercise works. As with many of the audio tracks that come with this book, I demonstrate with the exercise the first time through, and you take over for the second pass.

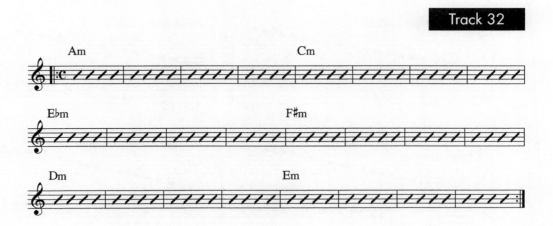

Once you can get through these six keys with the practice track using harmonic minor scale pattern 1, go back and memorize the same sequence using patterns 2, 3, and 4.

Next go through the exercise focusing on one pattern at a time until you can get through the entire exercise using each of the four moveable harmonic minor scale patterns.

Once you can get through this exercise using the four moveable harmonic minor patterns without mistakes, try using only open position harmonic minor scales and even one-string harmonic minor scales. Good luck!

Opening up: Harmonic minor scales in open position

The following figure shows all the available notes in each of the 12 harmonic minor scales while staying in open (first) position. Notice that these scales extend beyond one octave and also include partial scale segments that extend higher or lower, covering the entire range of open position.

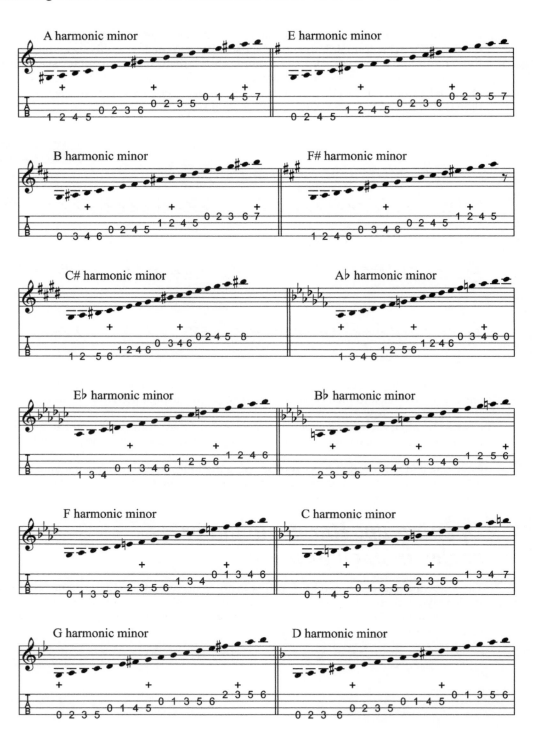

When you're comfortable with these open-scale positions, try incorporating some of the scale sequences from throughout this book by memorizing a sequence and applying it to the open position scale patterns.

Figuring out the fingerboard: Harmonic minor scales on one string

Practicing scales on one string is a great way to discover the upper ranges of the fingerboard. Pay close attention to the fingerings, shifting where indicated. The following figure shows the one-string pattern for the E harmonic minor scale, which starts on the second fret of the d-string.

When working on one string scales, be aware that they are really only two tetrachords separated by a whole step or two frets. See Chapter 2 for some tetrachords warm-up exercises.

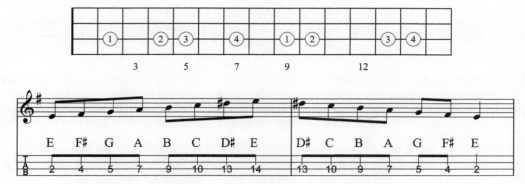

Pondering Moveable Melodic Minor Scale Patterns

The melodic minor scale uses different notes when *ascending* (going up) than when *descending* (going down), which makes this scale a little difficult to learn and memorize. Ascending, the melodic minor scale is simply a major scale with a lowered third. (In the other minor scales, the sixth and seventh steps are altered.) Descending, the melodic minor scale is a major scale with lowered third, sixth, and seventh steps.

Melodic minor scale pattern 1

Melodic minor scale pattern 1 starts with your first finger on the root note of the scale and finishes with your fourth finger on the octave. This pattern uses two strings on the mandolin. You can play it anywhere on the neck, depending on which minor key you're practicing.

The following figure shows the E melodic minor scale pattern 1 as a neck diagram, standard sheet music, and tab. I indicate the lowered sixth and seventh steps of the descending scale with squares in the neck diagram. To play this pattern, place your first finger on the E note, which is on the second fret of the d-string, and follow the neck diagram and tab, paying close attention to the suggested fingerings. Track 33 shows how it's done.

The melodic minor scale is different going up from that going down. Watch the sixth and seventh steps carefully.

Track 33

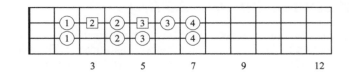

Now practice the G melodic minor scale (see the following figure and listen to Track 34) by moving the previous pattern up three frets, placing your first finger on the G note at the fifth fret of the d-string. This sequence uses alternate picking and 16th notes (semiquavers), which means that you need to play four notes (two down and two up) for each click of your metronome.

Have a go at practicing the scale sequence in all 12 keys, by simply placing your first finger on the root note of your choice and playing the melodic minor pattern 4.

Track 34

Melodic minor scale pattern 2

Melodic minor scale pattern 2 starts with your second finger on the root note of the scale and finishes with your first finger on the octave. This pattern uses three strings on the mandolin. You can play it anywhere on the neck, depending on which scale you're practicing.

The following figure shows the G melodic minor scale pattern 2 as a neck diagram, standard sheet music, and tab. To play this pattern, place your second finger on the G note, which is on the fifth fret of the d-string. For a demo, flip to Track 35.

The G melodic minor scale pattern 2 sounds the same as the G melodic minor scale in pattern 1: same sound, different fingering.

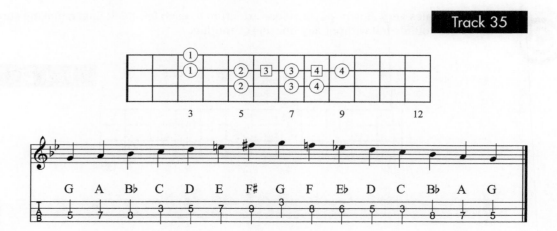

 Now try your hand at practicing the F melodic minor scale by moving the G melodic minor pattern 2 down by two frets, placing your second finger on the F note at the third fret of the d-string, and using the scale sequence in the following figure. The sequence uses triplets played with all down-strokes. Listen to Track 36 to hear this sequence.

 Try this scale sequence in all 12 keys: simply place your second finger on the root note of your choice and play this melodic minor pattern 2 sequence.

Melodic minor scale pattern 3

Melodic minor scale pattern 3 starts with your third finger on the root note of the scale and finishes with your second finger on the octave. This pattern uses three strings on the mandolin. You can play it anywhere on the neck, depending on which scale you're practicing.

 The following figure shows the A melodic minor scale pattern 3 as a neck diagram, standard sheet music, and tab. To play this pattern, place your third finger on the A note, which is on the seventh fret of the d-string, following the neck diagram and tab to ensure proper fingerings. Track 37 gives you a demo.

Practice scales very slowly, paying close attention to each left-hand finger, making sure that each note sounds full without any buzzing or muting.

Track 37

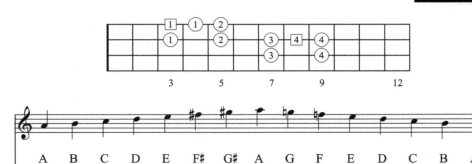

You can transpose this pattern to the key of D melodic minor (see the following figure) by moving it over by one string (lower) so that the first note is now the seventh fret of the g-string. Play the sequence with tremolo. Listen to Track 38 to hear an eight stroke per quarter note (crotchet) tremolo.

Eight tremolo strokes are really only four down and four up. If you're having trouble keeping the strokes in time, try omitting the up-stroke, making four down-strokes per quarter note. When you can keep in time, add the up-strokes to complete the tremolo.

Track 38

Try the following scale sequence in all 12 keys, by simply placing your third finger on the root note of your choice and playing this melodic minor pattern 3 sequence.

Melodic minor scale pattern 4

Melodic minor scale pattern 4 starts with your fourth finger on the root note of the scale and finishes with your third finger on the octave. This pattern uses three strings on the mandolin. You can play it anywhere on the neck, depending on which scale you're practicing.

The following figure shows the D melodic minor scale pattern 4 as a neck diagram, standard sheet music, and tab. To play this pattern, place your fourth finger on the D note, which is on the seventh fret of the g-string, following the suggested fingerings in the neck diagram and tab. You can hear this pattern on Track 39.

I show the D melodic minor scale in two ways. Make sure that when you play the D melodic minor scale pattern 3 in the section 'Melodic minor scale pattern 3', it sounds the same as this D melodic minor scale pattern 4, just with different fingering.

Track 39

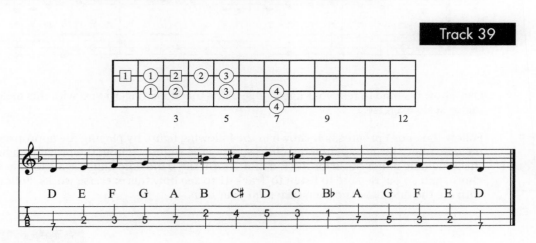

Now try your hand at practicing the B♭ melodic minor scale by moving the previous pattern to the eighth fret of the d-string (see the following figure). Be sure to follow the pick direction markings above the tab. To hear this played, listen to Track 40.

Track 40

Practice the scale sequence in all 12 keys by simply placing your fourth finger on the root note of your choice and playing this melodic minor pattern 4 sequence.

The following figure shows a simple melodic minor scale sequence in the key of B minor using melodic minor scale pattern 1. Memorize this sequence. Try playing this sequence in other keys by moving the major scale pattern up or down a few frets or even over to the adjacent string keeping in mind that the root note or the name of the scale will be played with your first finger. You can hear this simple sequence in the following exercise.

Okay, now it's time to test your knowledge of the mandolin fingerboard with this melodic minor scale exercise.

Follow the chord progression shown in the following figure by playing the appropriate melodic minor scale to match the chords, using the sequence from the previous figure. Play the B melodic minor scale for the B minor chord, the D melodic minor scale for the D minor chord, and so on. Be sure to listen to Track 41 to see how this exercise works. Follow along with me the first time and then take it on your own.

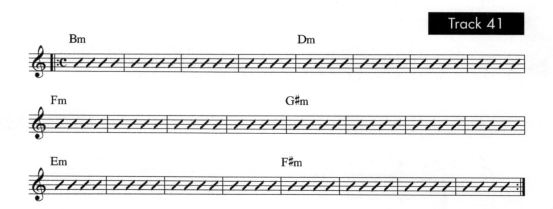

Track 41

Once you can get through these six keys with the practice track using pattern 1, go back and memorize the same sequence using patterns 2, 3, and 4.

Next go through the exercise focusing on one pattern at a time until you can get through the entire exercise using each of the four moveable melodic minor scale patterns.

Once you can get through this exercise using the four moveable melodic minor patterns without mistakes, try using only open position melodic minor scales and even one-string melodic minor scales. Good luck!

Opening things up with melodic minor scales in open position

The following figure shows all the available notes in each of the 12 melodic minor scales while staying in open (first) position. Notice that these scales extend beyond one octave and also include partial scale segments that extend higher or lower, covering the entire range of open position.

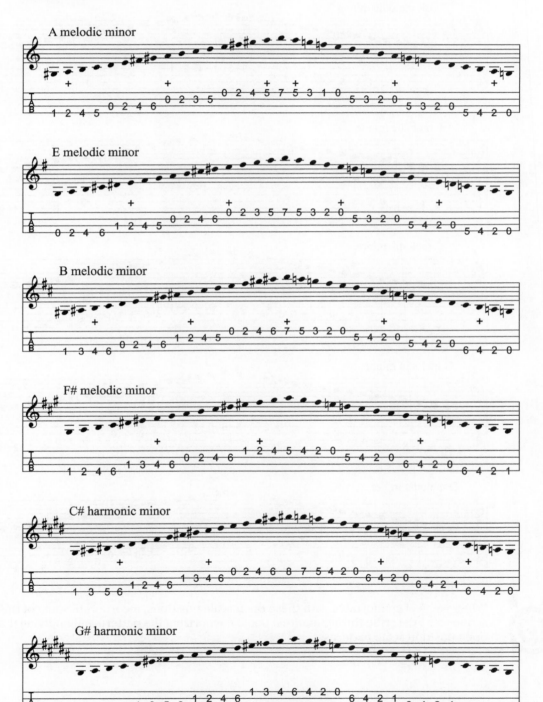

Eb melodic minor

Bb melodic minor

F melodic minor

C melodic minor

G melodic minor

D melodic minor

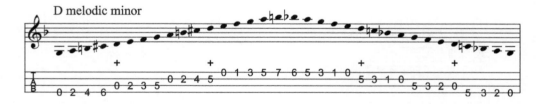

When you feel comfortable with these open-scale positions, incorporate some of the scale sequences I describe throughout this book, memorizing the pattern and applying it to the open position scale patterns.

Figuring out the fingerboard: Melodic minor scales on one string

Practicing scales on one string allows you to discover the upper ranges of the fingerboard. Pay close attention to the fingerings, shifting where indicated. The following figure shows the one-string pattern for the E melodic minor scale, which starts on the second fret of the d-string.

You can move these patterns up the neck and also from string to string in the same way as all the scales I discuss in this chapter are moveable. Just remember that wherever you place your first finger is the new root note of the scale.

Chapter 5

Bringing Color to Your Playing with Pentatonic and Chromatic Scales

In This Chapter

▶ Playing patriotically with the so-called Americana scale

▶ Keeping your spirits up with the blues scale

▶ Steeling yourself to play chromatic passages

*I*n this chapter I introduce you to pentatonic and chromatic scales. Pentatonic scales are simply major or minor scales with a few notes removed. Two notes to be exact. Chromatic scales on the other hand contain all 12 notes. For example a chromatic scale on one string would include every fret.

Pentatonic scales are derived from major and minor scales. These scales can be useful when you're improvising or if you play *by ear* (meaning that you don't read music but develop your musical skills by listening and imitating). Pentatonic scales feature prominently in ancient music from around the world and in modern music such as blues, country, and rock and roll.

You can transform major and minor pentatonic scales by adding one additional note outside the key note (called a *blue note*). This blue note can present a few playing challenges, because in some cases you need to use three consecutive frets (what's called a *chromatic passage*). Complete chromatic scales themselves don't appear in any specific types of music, and there is no chromatic key, but chromatic passages of three or four notes or more are common in blues, jazz, bluegrass, ragtime, and some classical music. I supply you with two common ways of handling chromatic scales and passages on the mandolin.

Listen to the demonstration tracks *before* you try to play the licks in this chapter (or any music for that matter). Imitation is the best way to learn music, and so listen first and then with the help of the notation and tablature (tab), aim to match the sound of the track. If you haven't downloaded the all-important audio portion of this book yet, now's the perfect time. The audio files are available at www.dummies.com/go/mandolinexercises.

Jammin' With Moveable Major Pentatonic Scales

Moveable major pentatonic scales are nothing more than moveable major scale patterns with the fourth and seventh steps removed. These moveable major pentatonic scales come in the same four varieties as moveable major scale patterns: pattern 1 starts with finger one, pattern 2 with finger two, and so on. If you're not yet quite up to speed on your major scale patterns, spend some time working with Chapter 3.

In this section I demonstrate the four moveable major pentatonic patterns and open position major pentatonic patterns, each pattern includes a variation that transforms the major pentatonic scale into the Americana scale which is simply a major pentatonic with the addition of one outside of the key note which happens to be the flatted third or minor third. This outside of the key note is called a blue note. The traditional major pentatonic has an old world sound that may conjur up images of the Orient or possible native American wooden flutes. It is also the scale of many folk melodies and simple gospel songs. By adding the blue note to the major pentatonic you create a sound with major and minor qualities. This ambiguous sound is a major ingredient in honky-tonk, bluegrass, country and western, rock and roll, blues, jazz, and most forms of music developed in America. I provide two audio versions of each pattern, so you can hear the difference. This scale doesn't have a common established name, and so I call it the *Americana* scale because it's such a staple ingredient of many of the music forms included in the Americana genre.

Major pentatonic scale pattern 1

Major pentatonic scale pattern 1 is based on major scale pattern 1 from Chapter 3. You start pattern 1 with your first finger on the root note and finish at the octave with your fourth finger; only two strings are required to play the complete one-octave scale.

The following figure shows the tab, standard notation, and a neck diagram for the major pentatonic and Americana scale pattern 1. A glance at the neck diagram reveals that in the Americana version of this scale, you play two notes in a row with your third finger. I indicate the blue note (or outside of the key note) in the neck diagram with a square instead of a circle and with parentheses in the notation and tab.

Listen to Track 42 for a demonstration of the E major pentatonic scale using pattern 1 followed by the E Americana scale using pattern 1. Notice how the addition of one note changes the overall mood of the scale.

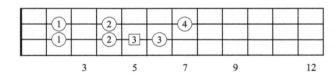

I suggest that when playing the Americana version of this scale, you use a slide from the minor third (the blue note) to the major third; that is, pick the blue note (the third note in the scale) and then slide to the next note without picking it. The result is a type of slur that helps define the ambiguous sound of this scale.

Many instrumentalists and vocalists bend the blue note up to the major note. Bending strings from one pitch to another on a mandolin is difficult, however, and therefore a less common technique.

After each of the four moveable major pentatonic scale patterns in this chapter, I provide a little melody which uses the major pentatonic scale. These can be considered *licks:* phrases that you can add to your mandolin vocabulary. Remember that these licks are all built from moveable scale patterns, meaning that by moving these licks to different locations on the fingerboard you're able to play them in any key.

The following lick uses *double stops* (two notes played at the same time) and slides. It also features a technique called *bridging,* where you hold down two strings, in this case the d- and a-strings, with one finger (your first finger). Listen to this lick on Track 43 before you try to play it.

Track 43

Major pentatonic scale pattern 2

Major pentatonic scale pattern 2 is based on major scale pattern 2 from Chapter 3. For pattern 2, you start with your second finger on the root note and finish at the octave with your first finger; three strings are required to play the complete scale. As the neck diagram shows, the Americana version of this scale requires you to play two notes in a row with your fourth finger, which requires a slide (a good test of the strength of your fourth finger).

Check out Track 44 for a demonstration of the G major pentatonic scale using pattern 2 followed by the G Americana scale using pattern 2.

Track 44

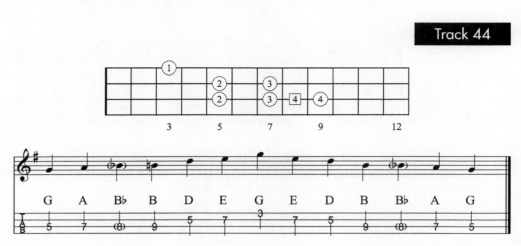

The following pattern 2 G major lick starts with your first finger on the G note, which is at the third fret of the e-string and is played with an up-stroke. Be sure to follow the pick direction marked above the tab.

Listen carefully to Track 45 for this syncopated lick. Syncopated means accents are on the off-beat. Get the sound of it in your head before having a go yourself.

Track 45

Major pentatonic scale pattern 3

You start major pentatonic scale pattern 3 with your third finger on the root note and finish at the octave with your second finger, thus three strings are required to play the complete scale. If you look at the neck diagram you can see that the Americana version of this scale requires you play two notes in a row with your first finger, which requires a slide.

Track 46 demonstrates the A major pentatonic scale using pattern 3 followed by the A Americana scale using pattern 3.

Track 46

The next lick in A major sounds like a standard bluegrass mandolin lick. Pattern 3 is a position that's commonly called the *chop* position, because it's used when chording to produce the backbeat (or chop) sound in bluegrass.

Listen to this major pentatonic pattern 3 lick on Track 47 before you try to play it.

Major pentatonic scale pattern 4

To play major pentatonic scale pattern 4, you start with your fourth finger on the root note and finish at the octave with your third finger; three strings are therefore required to play the complete scale. The neck diagram shows that in the American version of this scale, you play two notes in a row with your second finger, requiring a slide.

Listen to Track 48, which demonstrates the D major pentatonic scale using pattern 4 followed by the D Americana scale using pattern 4.

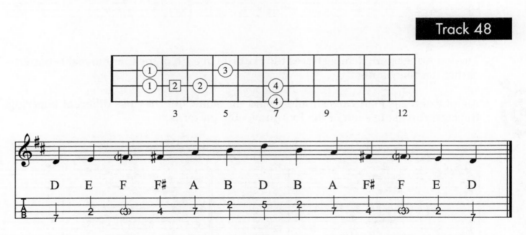

You play the next lick in the key of D major with pattern 4. It sounds a bit like a boogie-woogie bass line or maybe a rhythm section part from an early Elvis Presley song. You can hear this lick on Track 49.

Playing the greatest country lick of all time

Lester Flatt was a bluegrass guitarist and singer who performed with Bill Monroe in the original Bluegrass Boys. He and Earl Scruggs left Monroe's band in 1948 and went on to have much success with the bluegrass group The Foggy Mountain Boys. One of Lester Flatt's signature guitar licks became known as the Flatt run (or the G run, because it's based on the standard G chord form which is common in bluegrass guitar playing). This lick is a staple in many forms of country music and is used as a basis for improvisation.

Take a look at the following figure for the 'Flatt' run played on the mandolin using Americana scale pattern 1 in the key of E. You can hear this very recognizable lick on Track 50.

Track 50

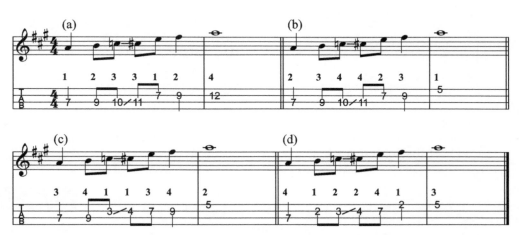

The following figure demonstrates the Flatt run in each of the four moveable patterns I discuss earlier in this chapter.

All four of these Flatt runs should sound the same, but they use different fingerings. Practice the Flatt run using each of the four moveable patterns.

Okay, now I want to test your knowledge of the fingerboard using the four major pentatonic scale patterns with this exercise. Follow the chord progression in the following figure by playing the Flatt run to match the chords. Using pattern 1, play the A run twice for the A chord, the C run twice for the C chord, and so on.

Be sure to listen to Track 51 to see how this exercise works. This track has you playing with a honky-tonk band with the rhythm section playing in a traditional country style. When you can get through these six keys with the practice track using pattern 1, go back and memorize the Flatt run using patterns 2, 3, and 4. Next go through the exercise focusing on one pattern at a time until you can get through the entire exercise using each of the four moveable major scale patterns.

Track 51

When you've mastered the Flatt run, have a go at playing the four closed pattern major pentatonic licks I describe earlier in this section and try to fit them over Track 51. The rhythm section is in the left speaker and the mandolin on the right. Isolate the rhythm section and make the mandolin track fade out by adjusting your balance control for the left speaker.

Pickin' up a storm with major pentatonic scales in open position

As with learning other scales and arpeggios, mastering pentatonic scale patterns in open position is extremely important when you're developing as a mandolin player. The following figure shows all 12 major pentatonic scales in open position. The blue note that transforms the major pentatonic scale into the Americana scale is in parentheses. The root note of each scale in indicated with a + placed directly above the tablature.

Make the effort to memorize the names of the notes along with the patterns on the mandolin; it's very important to achieving a good understanding of the instrument. Notes are like people: they like it when you remember their names!

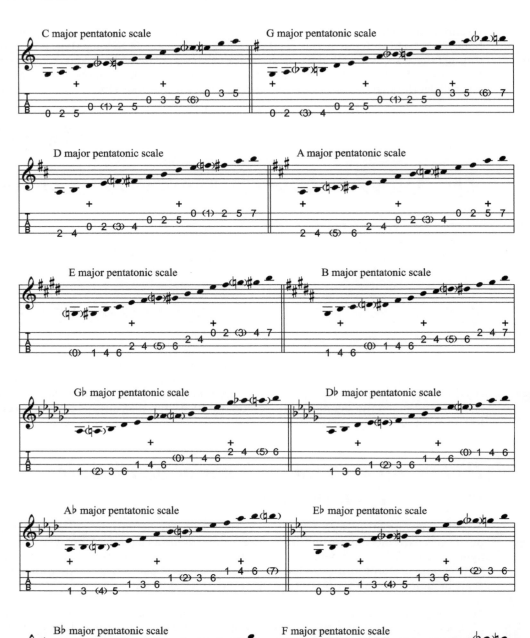

Is it a bird, is it a plane? Is it a scale, is it an arpeggio?

Pentatonic scales are a bit different from the major and minor scales I describe in Chapters 3 and 4: they don't function as complete keys where chords are built from each note of the scale to make diatonic harmony (which I demonstrate in Chapters 12 and 13). Major and minor pentatonic scales are very useful for the improvising mandolin player who enjoys playing blues, rock and roll, jazz, bluegrass, or any other musical style requiring improvisation or the ability to play by ear. A simple method would be to simply improvise using the G major pentatonic scale when you are playing in the key of G major. Another method of using pentatonic scales while improvising is to use a separate pentatonic scale for each chord in a song or chord progression, such as you would with arpeggios.

You can see these scales as being like extended arpeggios, meaning that they have more notes in them than the chord has.

For example, take a look at the G major chord, which contains the notes G, B, and D. The G major pentatonic scale contains the notes G, A, B, D, and E. The A and E notes add color to the arpeggio and also make it easier to invent melodies. Many of the world's catchiest melodies or riffs are simply pentatonic scales, such as 'Angelina Baker' (fiddle tune), 'Amazing Grace' (gospel standard) and 'Voodoo Child' (Jimi Hendrix song). From music around the world to gospel music to rock and roll, pentatonic scales have existed for thousands of years and are unlikely to fall out of style any time soon.

The following figure demonstrates the Flatt run from the preceding section using open strings whenever possible for the keys of A, G, D, and C. When you're comfortable with these open positions, go back to Track 51 and practice the Flatt run using open strings when possible.

The following figure shows a mandolin solo that a musician could have improvised based on the notes in the Flatt run using a standard chord progression in the key of G major. By thinking of the Flatt run as an arpeggio instead of a scale, and applying it to a common chord progression, you'll eventually be able to make up some extremely cool major key licks or complete solos.

Listen to Track 52 first and try to hear the scales being used as extended arpeggios, meaning a different pentatonic scale used for each chord and then learn the solo and play along. Remember that the mandolin track is muted the second time, leaving only the mid tempo bluegrass rhythm track for you to play with.

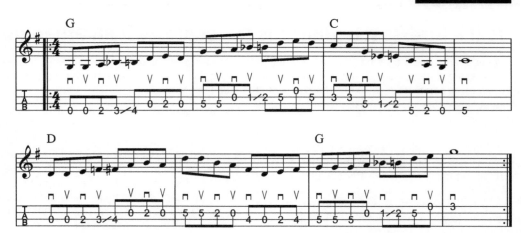

Here is another example of a short solo but this time in the key of D major, using an Americana scale for each chord.

Listen to Track 53 and then play the following solo. When you can play this exercise and the previous one cleanly, try to improvise a solo using Tracks 52 and 53 as backing tracks. You can mute the mandolin track, leaving only the bluegrass style rhythm section, by selecting playback from the left speaker alone.

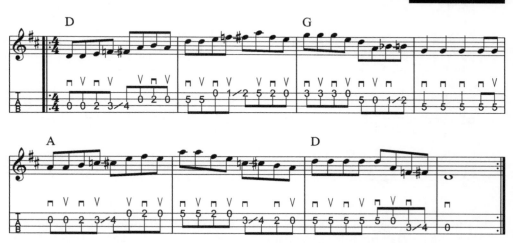

Rockin' with Moveable Minor Pentatonic Scales

Moveable minor pentatonic scales are just moveable natural minor scale patterns with the second and sixth steps removed. You find them in the same four varieties as moveable minor scale patterns. Pattern 1 starts with finger one, pattern 2 with finger two, and so on. To make sure that you're confident with minor scale patterns, check out Chapter 4.

In this section I demonstrate the four moveable minor pentatonic patterns and open position minor pentatonic patterns, each pattern includes a variation that transforms the minor pentatonic scale into the blues scale which is simply a minor pentatonic with the addition of one outside of the key note which happens to be the flatted fifth. This outside of the key note is called a blue note. Like the major pentatonic scale, the minor pentatonic has an old world sound that you may recognize from songs like the gospel standard "Poor Wayfaring Stranger" which by the way is in *Mandolin for Dummies* or the epic Jimi Hendrix guitar riff used in "Voodoo Child." I provide two audio versions of each pattern, so you can hear the difference. By adding the flatted fifth (a blue note) to the minor pentatonic, you have a sound that's quintessential to blues, jazz, and rock music, called the *blues* scale. Although primarily thought of as a minor type of scale that works well with minor chords, in some situations this minor scale sounds right for styles of music played over major chords.

The blues scale is the cornerstone of most classic rock lead-guitar playing and can also be a very valuable tool when improvising or creating a mandolin solo.

I indicate the blue note (the outside-of-the-key note) in each of the following minor pentatonic blues scales with a square for the neck diagrams and with parentheses for the notation and tab.

Minor pentatonic scale pattern 1

Minor pentatonic scale pattern 1 starts with your first finger on the *root note* (or name) of the scale and finishes with your fourth finger on the *octave* (or higher root) note. This pattern uses two strings on the mandolin, and you can play it anywhere on the neck, depending on which minor pentatonic scale you're practicing.

The following figure shows the E minor pentatonic scale in a neck diagram, standard sheet music, and tab. To play this pattern, place your first finger on the E note (on the second fret of the d-string) and follow the neck diagram and tab, making sure you use the suggested fingerings. By looking at the neck diagram, you can see that when playing the blues scale, you will need to play two notes in a row with your first finger, requiring a slide.

Listen to Track 54 for a demonstration of the E minor pentatonic scale using pattern 1, followed by the E blues scale using pattern 1.

Track 54

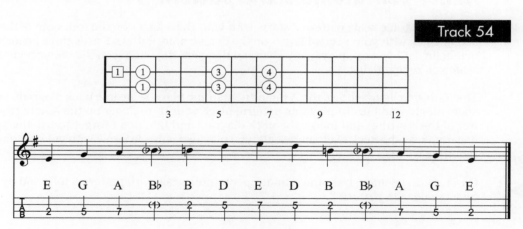

Minor pentatonic scale pattern 2

Start this minor pentatonic scale pattern with your second finger on the root note of the scale and finish with your first finger on the octave note. The pattern uses three strings on the mandolin; you can play it anywhere on the neck, depending on which minor pentatonic scale you are practicing.

The following figure shows the G minor pentatonic blues scale in a neck diagram, standard sheet music, and tab. Place your second finger on the G note (located on the fifth fret of the d-string) and follow the neck diagram and tab, making sure that you use the suggested fingerings. In this example, your first finger is responsible for the slide. Remember that finger one is your strongest finger, and easier for sliding than finger two; similarly, finger two is stronger than finger three, and so on.

Listen to Track 55 for the G minor pentatonic scale and the G blues scale using pattern 2.

Track 55

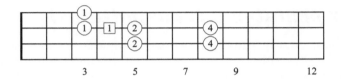

Minor pentatonic scale pattern 3

Minor pentatonic scale pattern 3 starts with your third finger on the root note of the scale and finishes with your second finger on the octave note. Pattern 3 uses three strings on the mandolin, and you can play it anywhere on the neck, depending on the minor pentatonic scale you're practicing.

The following figure shows the A minor pentatonic blues scale in a neck diagram, standard sheet music, and tab. To play this pattern, place your third finger on the A note (the seventh fret of the d-string) and follow the neck diagram and tab; don't forget to use the suggested fingerings. As the neck diagram reveals, you play two notes in a row with your second finger, requiring a slide.

On Track 56 I demonstrate the A minor pentatonic scale with pattern 3 followed by the A blues scale with pattern 3.

Track 56

A C D E♭ E G A G E E♭ D C A

Minor pentatonic scale pattern 4

Start minor pentatonic scale pattern 4 with your fourth finger on the root note and finish with your third finger on the octave. This pattern uses three strings on the mandolin. You can play this scale anywhere on the neck, depending on which minor pentatonic scale you're practicing.

The following figure shows the D minor pentatonic scale in a neck diagram, standard sheet music, and tab. To play this pattern, place your fourth finger on the D note (on the seventh fret of the g-string) and follow the neck diagram and tab, making sure you use the suggested fingerings. As the neck diagram shows, you play two notes in a row with your third finger, requiring a slide.

Listen to Track 57 for a demonstration of the D minor pentatonic scale using pattern 4 followed by the D blues scale using pattern 4. Notice that in pattern 4, you don't use your first and strongest finger at all and that the pattern is the same as pattern 3, where you do use your stronger fingers. This is a good argument for just playing pattern 3 by moving your hand up one position or two frets and using your stronger fingers.

Track 57

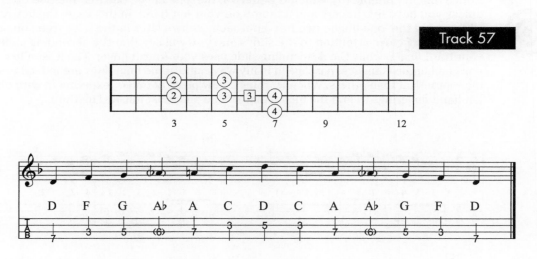

D F G A♭ A C D C A A♭ G F D

Breaking the fingering rules

Sometimes we need to break the rules or at least invent new ways of doing things. Standard mandolin fingering which is reviewed in Chapter 1, has been the method used so far for all of the scale patterns and sequences shown so far in this book. The Americana and blues versions of these pentatonic scales present an interesting challenge in that they contain a chromatic passage consisting of three consecutive frets. For example; the G blues scale contains the notes G, B♭, C, D♭, D, and F. Notice that the notes C, D♭, and D are what is called a chromatic passage because the three notes are all one half step or one fret apart. In the previous examples in this chapter, one finger would handle two of the notes by sliding from one to the other and another finger would handle the third note of the chromatic passage. Instead of using slides to handle the chromatic passages, another option is to use a separate finger for each note. While this is a variation on traditional fingerings, I wouldn't worry about the mandolin police paying you a visit. More on chromatic passages and the complete chromatic scale later in this chapter. The following blues scale lick uses the 'one finger, one fret' fingering method I describe in the later section 'One fret, one finger' to handle the chromatic passage.

Listen to Track 58 and then try to play this simple lick using the blues scale.

Track 58

The following figure demonstrates the same blues scale lick in each of the four moveable minor pentatonic scale patterns I have already demonstrated. Practice the lick using each of the four moveable patterns.

Notice that in example (d), which is pattern 4, the 'one finger, one fret' method doesn't work unless you have five fingers and a thumb on your left hand. In this case, the lick requires slides using the 'one finger, two fret' approach (shown later in the 'Two frets, one finger' section). Pay close attention to the slides and you will see that the ascending slide uses your third finger, while the descending slide uses your fourth finger. The lesson here is that you can handle a musical passage in many ways, and some fingerings are indeed easier and more practical than others. When learning a new piece of music, experiment with different left-hand fingerings to find the most comfortable and most musical method.

Now you get the chance to test your knowledge of the mandolin fingerboard using moveable minor pentatonic scale patterns with the next exercise. Follow the chord progression shown in the following figure by playing the lick from the preceding figure to match the chords.

This track finds you playing this blues scale lick while the rhythm section is laying down a shuffle beat sounding a bit like a lost episode of the *Pink Panther* cartoon. Be sure to listen to Track 59 to see how this exercise works. I play the exercise along with the backing track the first time before dropping out and leaving you to go it alone. When you can get through these six keys with the practice track using pattern 1, go back and memorize the lick using patterns 2, 3, and 4. Next go through the exercise focusing on one pattern at a time until you can get through the entire exercise using each of the four moveable minor pentatonic scale patterns.

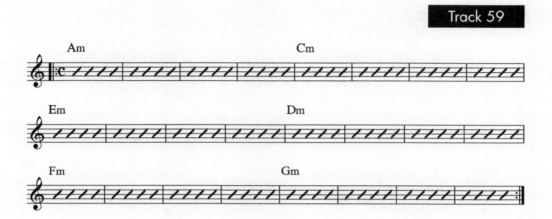

Track 59

Playin' the blues with minor pentatonic scales in open position

As I state throughout this book, learning all of your scales in open position is important. The following figure shows all 12 minor pentatonic scales in open position. I place the blue note that transforms the minor pentatonic scale into the blues scale in parentheses .

The following open position scales don't all start on the root note and may not sound like the desired scale if you simply start on the lowest note. To get the sound of the scale, locate the root note and play from the root note up to the next root note or the octave.

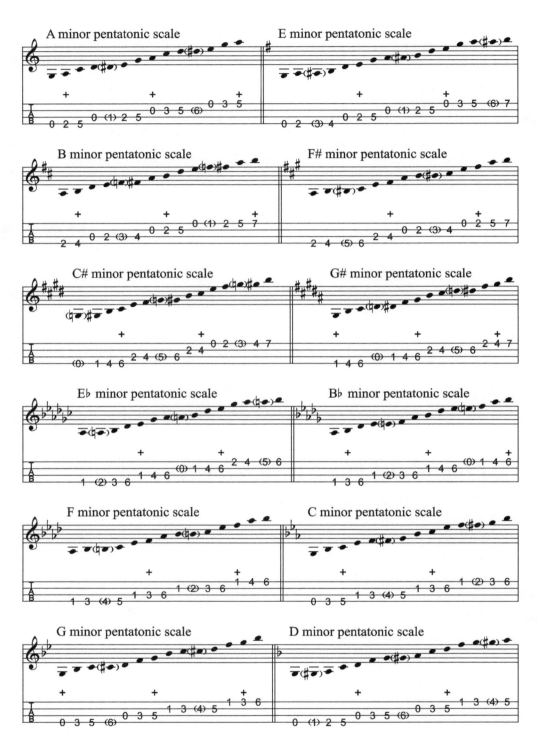

Employing a minor pentatonic blues scale over major chords

One of the most common uses for the blues scale is to use one scale over all three chords in a 12-bar blues chord progression. Even though the chords in a 12-bar blues are major or dominant chords, the blues scale based on the minor pentatonic scale fits very well over this common chord progression. Some people believe that the clash of major and minor at the same time is what give the blues its mournful sound. You find this concept of one minor pentatonic or blues scale played over an entire chord progression in blues, rock and roll, jazz, and bluegrass. The following figure demonstrates the G blues scale played over an entire 12-bar blues chord progression in the key of G major. Play this tune with all down-strokes. When you can play this tune, try your hand at improvising over the 12-bar blues using only the G blues scale, letting your ear guide you to notes that sound good.

Track 60 puts you in a Chicago style blues band playing a shuffle rhythm for this style of 12-bar blues.

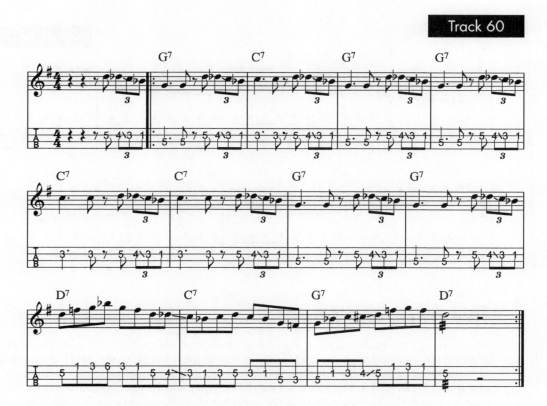

Discovering Two Ways of Handling Chromatic Scales

Chromatic scales consist of 12 half steps to the octave (in other words, all the notes). These scales, and even short *chromatic passages* (which require three or more consecutive frets), create challenges for the mandolin player, which you can handle in a number of ways. Persevering with them is worthwhile, because as you expand your repertoire, you will surely encounter tunes that use some form of chromaticism and are essential for genres such as blues, ragtime, jazz, and some classical music.

Here are the two basic techniques for chromatic scales:

- **Two frets, one finger:** The standard approach for mandolin, which requires some sliding in order to cover two frets with one digit
- **One fret, one finger:** A major departure from standard mandolin fingerings

I briefly explain each of these techniques. The techniques apply to long chromatic runs or smaller amounts of chromaticism, like you can see in the Americana and blues scales demonstrated throughout this chapter.

One fret, one finger

This approach is all about playing each note with a different left-hand finger and understanding where to shift from one region of four frets (one for each finger) to the next. Below is a chromatic scale exercise using the one fret, one finger method, including open strings when available.

Listen to Track 61 to hear this method of playing chromatic scales. Try this approach using all down-stokes.

Track 61

Two frets, one finger

Here I present the same exercise as in the section 'One fret, one finger', which uses standard mandolin fingering. This time, each finger is responsible for two frets, and I use open strings when possible. This method results in a whole lot of sliding or what is called the *same finger shift* which is covered in Chapter 6. When sliding you pick one note and slide or slur the second note (one pick stroke, two notes). In the same finger shift you pick each note. You should be familiar with both techniques.

Practicing your chromatic passages further

You have countless variations available when fingering chromatic passages, but most are simply a combination of the 'one fret, one finger' and 'two frets, one finger' approaches from the preceding sections. When you're comfortable with both techniques, experiment until the lick or musical passage not only sounds great but also feels good under your fingers.

The following one-string exercise is shown on the d-string, but I suggest you practice it on all four strings.

The key to this type of chromatic playing is shifting cleanly from one position to the other. Pay close attention to the ascending chromatic passages where the fourth-finger note is followed by a first finger; this shift is pretty tricky. The same applies for descending passages when shifting from a first-finger note to a fourth-finger note.

You can hear this one string, chromatic scale sequence on Track 62.

Track 62

0 1 2 1 2 3 4 1 2 3 4 1 2 1 2 1 2 1 4 3 2 1 4 3 2 1 2 1 0 1 0 1

0 1 2 3 4 5 6 7 8 9 10 11 12 11 12 11 12 11 10 9 8 7 6 5 4 3 2 1 0 1 0 1

Chapter 6

Connecting Scale Patterns to Extend Your Range

. . . .

In This Chapter

▶ Joining scale patterns while staying in position

▶ Trying out two different shifting techniques

. . . .

*E*xtending things is good: extending your skills, extending your circle of friends, extending your mandolin solos to interminable, prog-rock lengths . . . reducing your circle of friends again!

Most scale exercises are taught one octave at a time. Unfortunately, many tunes don't fit neatly into one octave. Learning how to transition smoothly from one octave to another is a necessary skill if you want to play many of the great tunes around. This chapter shows you some methods for connecting scale patterns so that you can stretch out luxuriously over two octaves.

Staying in Position while Extending Your Scales

Being able to access two octaves of a major or minor scale without shifting up or down the mandolin neck involves nothing more than connecting two (or more) patterns that you already know. As you discover in Chapters 3 and 4, each of these scales has four closed patterns that can be transposed or changed to any key simply by playing the pattern in a different place on the fingerboard. By following the simple principle of 'minus one' or 'plus one', you can easily connect scale patterns:

▶ **Ascending (going up) scale:** The second octave is the pattern that's one number lower than the first octave. For example, if you start the lower octave with pattern 3, the upper octave is pattern 2. If you start with pattern 2, the higher octave is pattern 1. Hence the name: 'minus one' pattern. Pattern 1 leads to pattern 4, which isn't really a lower number, but then only four patterns exist, so whatcha gonna do! All of these scale patterns are demonstrated in Chapter 3, Mastering Major Scales and Chapter 4 Discovering Three Types of Minor Scales.

▶ **Descending (going down) scale:** The opposite of the ascending scale is true here. If you're in pattern 1 on the higher strings of the mandolin and follow the scale down to the next octave, pattern 1 becomes pattern 2 as you move into the next lower octave. So if you're connecting a scale to a lower octave, the rule is 'plus one'. See Chapters 3 and 4 for more info on scale patterns.

Memorizing four crucial scale sequences

In this section I demonstrate four of the most helpful scale sequences you can memorize and practice. I demonstrate these sequences with major scales, but they can be applied to all three types of minor scales (natural, harmonic, and melodic; see Chapter 4 for details) as well. These patterns are simply a specific mathematical algorithm applied to a scale in both ascending and descending patterns.

That sounds a bit technical, and so think of these patterns as a repeating number sequence, where the numbers refer to the degree of the scale. For example, the sequence 1–3–2–4 in the key of A major represents the notes A–C♯–B–D; in A minor it would be A–C–B–D, and in G major it would be G–B–A–C.

Here are the four crucial practice sequences that you can apply to any scales:

- ✔ **Sequence 1:** Ascending 1–2–3–4–5–6–7–8 and so on; descending 8–7–6–5–4–3–2–1 and so on.
- ✔ **Sequence 2:** Ascending 1–2–3–1–2–3–4–2–3–4–5 and so on; descending 8–7–6–8–7–6–5–7–6–5–4 and so on.
- ✔ **Sequence 3:** Ascending 1–3–2–4–3–5–4–6–5–7 and so on; descending 7–5–6–4–5–3–4–2–3–1 and so on.
- ✔ **Sequence 4:** Ascending 1–2–3–4–2–3–4–5-3-4-5-6 and so on; descending 8–7–6–5–7–6–5–4–6–5–4–3 and so on.

Listen to Track 63 for a demonstration of these four crucial scale sequences played in the key of D major. Go to www.dummies.com/go/mandolinexercises for all the book's downloadable audio content.

Be sure to practice these crucial scale sequences repeatedly. Play each sequence a minimum of four times correctly, without stopping, before moving on.

Pattern 1 to pattern 4

The following figure shows a neck diagram of the A major scale, starting at the A note located at the second fret of the g-string, using pattern 1 for the lower octave and pattern 4 for the higher octave. Notice that I indicate the root notes with a square, while the other notes are in circles. See whether you can recognize the two patterns in this two-octave major scale. If not you may want to visit Chapter 3.

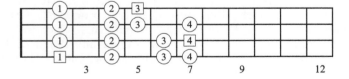

The following scale exercise is shown in the key of A major and uses major scale patterns 1 and 4 (see Chapter 3) along with crucial scale sequence 1 (from the section 'Memorizing four crucial scale sequences'). When you listen to Track 64, you can hear that the metronome is on beats two and four, or the *backbeat,* as I explain in Chapter 16. Learn to use your metronome in this way – you'll be grateful, and can thank me later.

Track 64

pattern 1   pattern 4   pattern 1

Pattern 2 to pattern 1

The following figure shows a neck diagram of the C major scale, starting at the C note located at the fifth fret of the g-string, using pattern 2 for the lower octave and pattern 1 for the higher octave. Can you recognize the two patterns from Chapter 3 in this two-octave major scale?

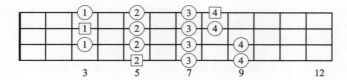

You can hear the following scale exercise on Track 65. It's in the key of C major and uses major scale patterns 2 and 1 (see Chapter 3) along with crucial scale sequence 2 (from the earlier section 'Memorizing four crucial scale sequences').

Pay attention to pick direction, because keeping a steady alternate picking pattern going may be trickier than you think.

Track 65

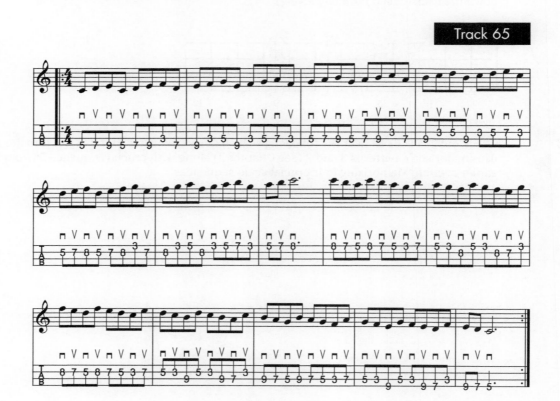

When you're comfortable with the four crucial scale exercises as written, try moving them up or down the fingerboard one fret at a time.

For example, play the entire exercise in the key of A major, which starts on the second fret of the g-string. When you've completed this exercise, move the pattern to the third fret of the g-string and play the exercise one fret higher, which is in the key of B♭. Play the complete exercise in B♭, starting at the third fret and playing the same patterns and sequence. After you finish the exercise, move it up one more fret, this time to the key of B (which is the fourth fret of the g-string).

Continue this pattern until the highest fret of the pattern is fret 12, and then reverse your direction and head on down the fingerboard one fret at a time until you run out of fingerboard at the nut.

Listen to Track 66 for a demonstration of this workout.

Pattern 3 to pattern 2

The following figure shows a neck diagram of the D major scale, starting at the D note located at the seventh fret of the g-string, using pattern 3 (see Chapter 3) for the lower octave and pattern 2 (see Chapter 3) for the higher octave.

Notice that pattern 2 is incomplete, extending only to the C♯ note at the ninth fret of the e-string. In order to reach the octave D, you'd need to shift again (unless you're one of those people who has an extra finger on your left hand). Also notice that I include two notes of the D scale that are below the root note because melodies do not just stop at the root note and as long as there are more scale notes and you have the fingers to play them you should learn them. By thinking this way you will have access to the most number of notes and the largest range without moving or shifting your left hand.

The aim is to be able to access as many notes of a scale as possible without shifting up or down the neck (called *position playing*).

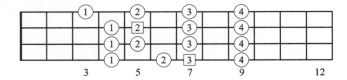

Check out Track 67 to hear the following scale exercise, which is in the key of D major and uses major scale patterns 3 and 2 (see Chapter 3) along with crucial sequence 3 (from the earlier section 'Memorizing four crucial scale sequences').

When you're confident that you have a good handle on left-hand major scale patterns and this set of four crucial practice sequences, try applying the same sequences to minor scales. Remember that the three types of minor scale are natural, harmonic, and melodic minor scales (see Chapter 4). Mastering all 12 of each type of minor scales using all these practice sequences should keep you busy for a while.

Listen to Track 68 for a demonstration of crucial sequence 2 (see the earlier section 'Memorizing four crucial scale sequences') applied to all three D minor scales: natural, harmonic, and melodic.

Pattern 4 to pattern 3

The following figure shows a neck diagram of the D major scale, starting at the D note located at the seventh fret of the g-string, using pattern 4 (see Chapter 3) for the lower octave and pattern 3 (see Chapter 3) for the higher octave.

Notice that pattern 3 in incomplete, extending only to the B note located at the seventh fret of the e-string. Also notice that I include three notes of the D scale that are below the root note. Because once again melodies do not always stop on the root note and you want to have as many notes of the scale under you fingertips and available if needed.

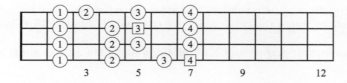

You can listen to the following scale exercise on Track 69. It's in the key of D major and uses major scale patterns 4 and 3 (see Chapter 3) along with crucial sequence 4 (from the earlier section 'Memorizing four crucial scale sequences').

Getting Shifty, Up and Down the Neck

Shifting is the technique of moving from one position or scale pattern to another. I divide shifting into two basic techniques: the same-finger shift and the two-finger shift. When you have these shifting techniques under your fingers, you're able to shift from any pattern or position on the neck to any other position or pattern.

Using the same-finger shift

I split the same-finger shift into two types:

- ✔ Picking each new note as you fret each note with the same left-hand finger.

- ✔ Slurring two notes together by using slides, where you pick the first note but not the second note of the slide. Slides and other slurs are covered in *Mandolin For Dummies*.

These two techniques can include any of your four left-hand fingers in an ascending and descending direction.

Performing the two-finger shift

I separate two-finger shifts into two types:

✔ **Low-numbered to high-numbered finger ascending, or the opposite for descending:** For example, 1–2, 1–3, 1–4, 2–3, 2–4, and 3–4 in an ascending direction or 4–3, 4–2, 4–1, 3–2, 3–1, and 2–1 in a descending direction.

✔ **High-numbered to low–numbered finger ascending, or the opposite for descending:** For example, 2–1, 3–1, 4–1, 3–2, 4–2, and 4–3 in an ascending direction or 3–4, 2–4, 1–4, 2–3, 1–3, and 1–2 in a descending direction.

Practicing shifting exercises

You perform the shifting exercises in this section on one string. If you're not up to speed on playing scales on one string, re-visit Chapters 3 and 4 to brush up.

The following figure, which I demonstrate on Track 70, shows six ways to play the same simple partial A major scale on one string using a variety of shifting possibilities. Examples (a)–(d) demonstrate four different ways to perform the one-finger shift, while examples (e)–(f) use two different types of two-finger shift. Pay attention to the finger numbers that are located above the tablature (tab).

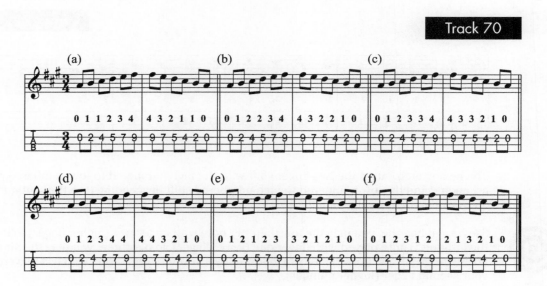

The following three exercises require you to use a few of the shifting techniques I cover earlier in this section. All three of the exercises use the D major scale on one string, starting on the open d-string note and extending to the 12th fret of the same string.

The first method uses the one-finger shift approach and applies it to the whole scale, meaning that you play the entire scale on one string using only one finger. Don't worry about playing fast here. Take things nice and slowly, making sure that each note is clear.

Listen to Track 71. The finger numbers above the tab suggest using finger one, which is a great place to start. But when you can do that, try using your other three fingers (one at a time) to practice the exercise.

Track 71

 The next exercise requires one shift on each of your four left-hand fingers.

When you're shifting with one finger, you can pick each note, or pick every other note and shift using a slide.

 See the following figure and Track 72 for this exercise that makes a one-finger shift for each of your four fingers.

Track 72

The next exercise uses the two-finger shift with the high-numbered to low-numbered shift ascending and the low-numbered to high-numbered shift descending (see the section 'Performing the two-finger shift').

See how in bar one, you play the fourth-fret F♯ note with finger two (higher finger) followed by the fifth-fret G note played with finger one (lower finger). In bar three, you play the ninth-fret B note with finger one (lower number) followed by a seventh-fret A note, which is played by your second finger (higher number).

You can hear this exercise on Track 73.

Track 73

A popular shift with bluegrass players, which works very well in the key of A (major or minor), is to slide up to the seventh fret with your third finger while playing a tune primarily in open position – an example of an ascending low number to high number, two-finger shift.

Notice that by sliding up to the seventh fret with your third finger, you're now in scale and arpeggio pattern 3 (see Chapters 3 and 7). This seventh fret note is in fact the next open string (the seventh fret of the d-string is A; the seventh fret of the a-string is E) and would normally be played open, but by sliding into the seventh fret while letting the next string ring open and picking both strings you get an interestingly bluesy unison or two strings playing the same note effect.

Hear this position-shift effect on Track 74.

Part III
Exploring Arpeggios

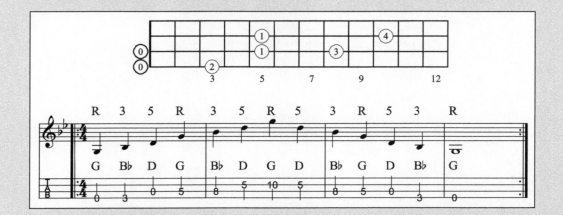

In this part . . .

✔ Take a glimpse into the world of arpeggios.

✔ Learn major, minor, seventh, major seventh, minor seventh, flat five, augmented and diminished arpeggios.

Chapter 7

Taking Notes One at a Time: Major Arpeggios

....

In This Chapter

▶ Majoring in four moveable major arpeggio patterns

▶ Playing all 12 major arpeggios in open position

▶ Practicing major arpeggios on one string

▶ Joining patterns to make two-octave arpeggios

....

Arpeggio isn't Pinocchio's brother, or a pasta sauce, or . . . no that's it, I'm out of Italian-based puns. *Arpeggio* is simply a word used to describe the notes of a chord played one at a time.

This chapter introduces you to four moveable (closed-position) major arpeggio forms along with open-position major arpeggios, major arpeggios on one string, and two-octave arpeggios.

Working on Moveable Major Arpeggios

Major arpeggios contain the root, third, and fifth notes of the major scale of the same name. For example, a C major arpeggio consists of the notes C, E, and G, which are the first, third, and fifth notes of the C major scale. Like when you're learning to play the major scales I describe in Chapter 3 using four moveable patterns, ideally you also need to be able to play major arpeggios on the mandolin using four moveable patterns. The name of each pattern corresponds with the finger that plays the root note of the arpeggio.

The following table shows the chord tones for each of the 12 major arpeggios.

Chord	Root	Third	Fifth
C	C	E	G
D♭	D♭	F	A♭
D	D	F#	A
E♭	E♭	G	B♭
E	E	G#	B
F	F	A	C
G♭	G♭	B♭	D♭
G	G	B	D
A♭	A♭	C	E♭
A	A	C#	E
B♭	B♭	D	F
B	B	D#	F#

Major arpeggio pattern 1

Pattern 1 is derived from major scale pattern 1 (from Chapter 3) and requires two strings to play the complete arpeggio. Start with your first finger on the root note and finish with your fourth finger on the octave.

Check out the following figure for notation, tablature (tab), and a neck diagram for the E major arpeggio pattern 1 and take a listen to the example on Track 75.

Track 75

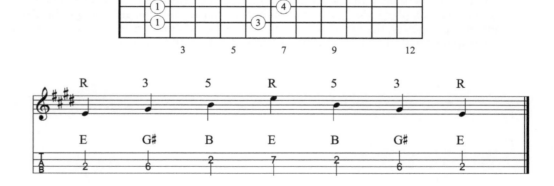

Major arpeggio pattern 2

Pattern 2 is based on major scale pattern 2 (check out Chapter 3) and requires three strings to play the complete arpeggio. You start with your second finger on the root note and finish with your first finger on the octave.

Look at the following figure for notation, tab, and a neck diagram for the G major arpeggio pattern 2, and turn your ears to the example on Track 76.

Track 76

Major arpeggio pattern 3

Pattern 3 comes from major scale pattern 3 (see Chapter 3) and requires three strings to play the complete arpeggio. You start with your third finger on the root note and finish with your second finger on the octave.

The following figure shows the notation, tab, and a neck diagram for the A major arpeggio pattern 3; take a listen to the example on Track 77 as well.

Track 77

Major arpeggio pattern 4

Pattern 4 is derived from major scale pattern 4 (check out Chapter 3) and requires three strings to play the complete arpeggio. It starts with your fourth finger on the root note and finishes with your third finger on the octave.

Pattern 4 is the same as pattern 3, but instead of using fingers one, two, and three, you use fingers two, three, and four: same shape, different fingers.

Follow the figure for notation, tab, and a neck diagram for the D major arpeggio pattern 3, and listen to the example on Track 78.

Track 78

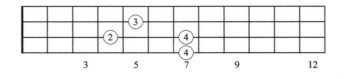

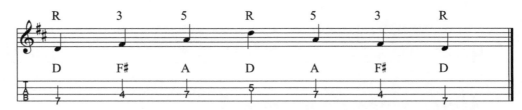

Moving major arpeggio patterns

The preceding major arpeggio patterns in this section are all *moveable,* meaning that you can move them up and down the neck and even across the strings to enable you to play any major arpeggio. For example, if you move the A major arpeggio up two frets, the same pattern becomes a B major arpeggio. Similarly, you can also move the A major arpeggio over one string (thicker) to make a D major arpeggio. The following figure shows the A major arpeggio using the four moveable patterns from earlier in this section: (a) pattern 1, (b) pattern 2, (c) pattern 3, and (d) pattern 4. Finger numbers are included above the tablature. Starting with pattern 1, memorize the simple sequence in all four patterns.

Next try to follow the chord progression in the following figure by playing the appropriate arpeggio to match the chords, using the simple arpeggio sequence from the previous figure. Be sure to listen to Track 79 to see how this exercise works. When you can get through these six keys with the practice track using pattern 1, well done! Your reward (!) is to memorize the same sequence using patterns 2, 3, and 4. Then go through the exercise focusing on one pattern at a time until you can get through the entire exercise. When you can get through this exercise using all four patterns in these six keys, sit back and enjoy your favorite beverage (maybe a nip of something strong if it's past 5 p.m. anywhere in the world).

The major arpeggio sequence is two measures in length with a repeat sign. The practice exercise chords last four measures each. By playing the sequence twice, you fill four measures.

`Track 79`

Be sure to download all the audio tracks for this book fro www.dummies.com/go/mandolinexercises. Hearing the examples is a sure way to discover whether you're playing them correctly. In all the arpeggio and scale exercise tracks, I play the exercise along with the backing track the first time through. The second time I drop out and then . . . you're up!

Staying in One Place: Major Arpeggios in Open Position

As they do with scales, mandolin players need to become familiar with all major arpeggios in open position (take them out for a nice dinner in a quiet restaurant – somewhere classy, nothing cheap – and see how you get on together; at least you have something in common – you're both into music). Open position is important because it uses open strings, which makes certain musical passages much easier.

Playing open strings on the mandolin is nothing to feel ashamed of. Even though the mandolin fingerboard is the same as the violin fingerboard, and classically trained violinists rarely if ever play open strings, open strings sound beautiful on the mandolin, so don't avoid them.

The following figure shows all 12 major arpeggios in open position.

When you have these open-position major arpeggios under your fingers, try applying them to the exercise on Track 79 (see the section 'Moving major arpeggio patterns'), but this time use only open-position major arpeggios.

Notice that some arpeggios contain open strings and some don't. The main rule with open position is that you play open strings when possible and don't go beyond the seventh fret for any notes.

Taking Leaps: Major Arpeggios on One String

One of the best ways to really discover the mandolin fingerboard is to practice arpeggios on one string. The first step is to know the names of the notes in each arpeggio. If you don't know them from memory yet, you can look them up in the chord tone figure at the beginning of the earlier 'Working on Moveable Major Arpeggios' section.

Here's how this exercise works: pick any major chord and determine the chord tones that make up the arpeggio: C major, for example. The chord tones for C major are the notes C, E, and G. Your job is to find these notes on each string as follows:

1. **Begin with the G note at the open g-string.**
2. **Play the C note at the fifth fret of the g-string with your third finger.**
3. **Play the E note at the ninth fret of the g-string with your first finger.**
4. **Play the G note at the 12 fret of the g-string with your third finger.**
5. **Play the arpeggio descending (down) using the same fingerings.**

When you have the C major arpeggio sounding clear on the g-string, move to the d-string following the same process. Remember that you won't be playing the same frets, but hunting down the same notes that are in the arpeggio.

Unlike the moveable arpeggio patterns from the earlier section 'Working on Moveable Major Arpeggios', one-string arpeggios don't have a consistent pattern when moving from string to string. This type of arpeggio playing relies on your knowledge of the chord tones and not on a geometric shape or pattern.

Continue working on the same arpeggio on the a-string and the e-string.

The following figure shows you a simple sequence for the C major arpeggio on each of the four strings: (a) g-string, (b) d-string, (c) a-string, and (d) e-string. This sequence can be found on Track 80 of the book's audio.

Note that the arpeggio doesn't need to start on the root note, just the lowest possible chord tone of the string you're working on.

Track 80

Connecting Major Arpeggio Patterns: Two Octaves

In this section I demonstrate a few common ways of playing two-octave major arpeggios. These examples include elements of open position and moveable major arpeggio patterns (see the earlier sections 'Staying in One Place: Major Arpeggios in Open Position' and 'Working on Moveable Major Arpeggios', respectively).

Although people have written complete books on nothing but position studies and shifts, I include just a few of the many possibilities. Chapter 8 has a few more two-octave shifting options. Feel free to explore beyond the examples presented in this chapter.

The following simple two-octave G major arpeggio sequence uses open position for the first octave, followed by a shift to *third position* (which requires you to place your first finger on the fifth fret of the d-string). The fifth fret is usually played by the third finger, hence the term 'third position'. Keep in mind that once you shift to third position you will be playing major arpeggio pattern 1 playing the G note with your first finger. Don't confuse positions with patterns. Look over the following figure for notation, tab, and a neck diagram for the two-octave G major 0-1 (open position followed by pattern 1) arpeggio.

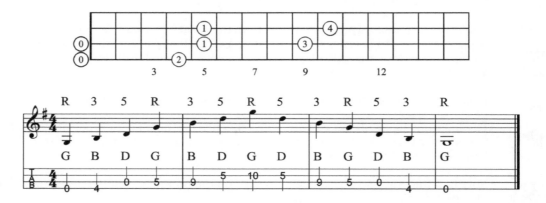

 Be sure to follow the proper fingerings. Finger numbers are the small numbers located inside the circles in the neck diagram. Proper fingerings are crucial for mastering these arpeggios.

You can play certain two-octave arpeggios on the mandolin while staying in open position, whereas others require a position shift. The A major arpeggio is one example of two full octaves in open position (which may explain why mandolin players like the key of A). Take a look at the following figure for notation, tab, and a neck diagram for the two-octave A major 1-0 arpeggio sequence.

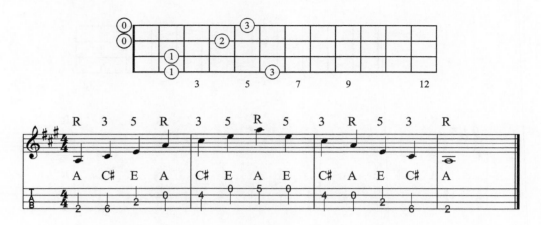

Notice how the second octave of the A arpeggio keeps the basic shape or form of pattern 1 but uses open strings, resulting in different fingering. The pattern 1-3 two-octave arpeggio uses pattern 1 for the lower octave and pattern 3 for the higher octave. You need to make a small position shift to play this two-octave arpeggio. The shift happens at the octave. Instead of using your fourth finger for the octave, which would be standard in pattern 1, slide your hand up the neck a little and play the octave with your third finger. This type of two finger shift is covered in Chapter 6. Now you're in position to play pattern 3 for the second octave of this two-octave arpeggio.

See the following figure for notation, tab, and a neck diagram for the two-octave A major arpeggio sequence using pattern 1 followed by pattern 3.

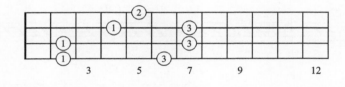

The pattern 1-4 two-octave arpeggio uses pattern 1 for the lower octave and pattern 4 for the higher octave. No position shift is needed to perform this two-octave arpeggio, but you do need a strong fourth finger.

See the following figure for notation, tab, and a neck diagram for the two-octave A major arpeggio sequence using pattern 1 followed by pattern 4.

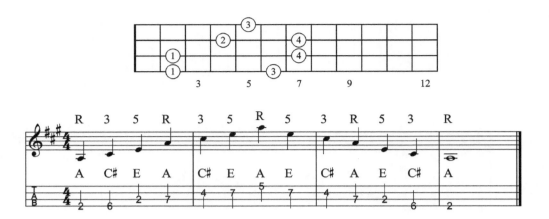

Notice that patterns 1-3 and 1-4 use the same notes played at the same frets with different fingerings. Pattern 1-3 requires a position shift, but pattern 1-4 doesn't. Remember that there's more than one way to skin a cat! Warning: don't try and skin a live cat – they don't like it and may scratch.

To test your two-octave major arpeggio skills, practice playing the simple two-octave arpeggio sequence that was used in the previous four figures, following the chord progression in the following figure. You can use any combination of open position, moveable patterns, or one-string arpeggios that you choose. The important thing is that you're able to follow the chords and keep up with the basic pop/rock beat on Track 81. Listen to Track 81 first, it is easier than I make it sound.

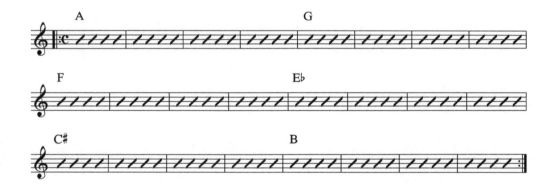

Chapter 8

Seeking Darkness: Minor Arpeggios

In This Chapter

▶ Playing four moveable minor arpeggio patterns

▶ Practicing all 12 minor arpeggios in open position

▶ Working on minor arpeggios on one string

▶ Stretching out over two-octave minor arpeggios

*L*ike the sad-sounding minor scales that I discuss in Chapter 4, here I present minor arpeggios on the mandolin in four closed patterns, in open position, and on one string (plus reaching over two octaves). However, for minor scales, unlike for minor arpeggios, you don't need to worry about learning three different types of minor chords (hurrah!), because no harmonic minor chords or melodic minor chords apply, only the scales from Chapter 4.

The difference between major arpeggios (see Chapter 7) and minor arpeggios is that the third of the chord is lowered by one half step, or one fret. (Remember that chords (arpeggios) contain the root, third, and fifth notes from a scale.) You alter minor arpeggios by flatting the third. For example, the C major chord contains the notes C, E, and G, whereas the C minor chord contains C, E♭, and G.

Going To the Dark Side: Moveable Minor Arpeggios

As you need to for the major arpeggios I show in Chapter 7, you need to practice minor arpeggios on the mandolin using four moveable patterns. The name of each pattern corresponds with which finger plays the root note of the arpeggio.

Memorizing the chord tones for every chord in every song you want to play seems like a lot of work – and is – but it's also a very good idea. I compare knowing these chord tones to the multiplication tables you learn at school. At the time it seemed silly to need to know the tables up to 12 times 12 from memory, but boy I'm glad I do. As an adult you realise why teachers drum these common multiplication answers into children: they come up many times in a day's normal activities. Imagine not knowing what 6 times 7 equals. For the same reason, in a normal day of musical activity, knowing the chord tones surely makes your life easier.

The following figure shows the chord tones for each of the 12 minor arpeggios.

Chord	Root	Third	Fifth
Cm	C	E♭	G
C#m	C#	E	G#
Dm	D	F	A
Ebm	E♭	G♭	B♭
Em	E	G	B
Fm	F	A♭	C
F#m	F#	A	C#
Gm	G	B♭	D
G#m	G#	B	D#
Am	A	C	E
Bbm	B♭	D♭	F
Bm	B	D	F#

Minor arpeggio pattern 1

Pattern 1 starts with your first finger on the root note and finishes with your fourth finger on the octave. See the following figure for notation, tablature (tab), and a neck diagram for E minor arpeggio pattern 1, and listen to the example on Track 82.

Track 82

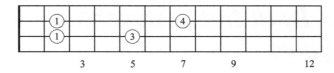

Minor arpeggio pattern 2

For pattern 2, start with your second finger on the root note and finish with your first finger on the octave. Check out the following figure for notation, tab, and a neck diagram for the G minor arpeggio pattern 2. You can find the example on Track 83 at www.dummies.com/go/ mandolinexercises.

Track 83

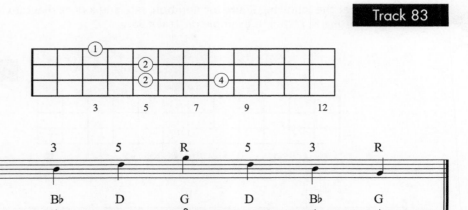

Minor arpeggio pattern 3

You start pattern 3 with your third finger on the root note and end up with your second finger on the octave. The following figure shows you notation, tab, and a neck diagram for the A minor arpeggio pattern 3. You can listen to the example on Track 84.

Track 84

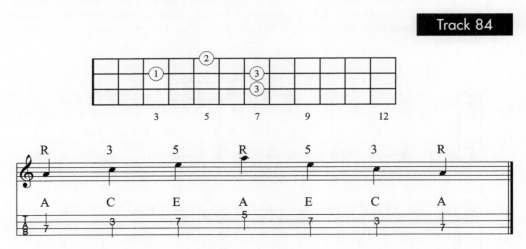

Minor arpeggio pattern 4

Pattern 4 starts with your fourth finger on the root note and finishes with your third finger on the octave. As with the major arpeggios in Chapter 7, pattern 4 is the same as pattern 3 in the preceding section. But instead of using fingers one, two, and three, you use fingers two, three, and four: same shape, different fingers.

In most cases I prefer to use pattern 3 when possible instead of using pattern 4, because my fourth finger isn't as strong as the other three. In some cases, however, you do need to use pattern 4.

Take a look at the following figure for notation, tab, and a neck diagram for the D minor arpeggio pattern 4. Listen to example on Track 85.

Track 85

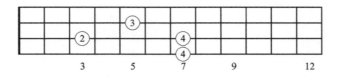

Moving minor arpeggio patterns

The following figure shows the A minor arpeggio using the four moveable patterns: (a) pattern 1; (b) pattern 2; (c) pattern 3; and (d) pattern 4. Starting with pattern 1, work on memorizing the simple sequence in all four patterns. The proper left hand fingerings are located directly above the tablature.

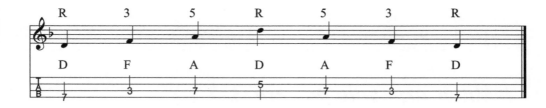

Practice the chord progression in the following figure by playing the simple minor arpeggio sequence from the previous figure (the one you just memorized). Start with pattern 1. Be sure to listen to Track 86 to see how this exercise works.

When you can complete the six keys in time with the practice track using only pattern 1, memorize the same sequence using patterns 2, 3, and 4. Next go through the exercise focusing on one pattern at a time until you can get through the entire exercise with each pattern without any mistakes.

The minor arpeggio sequence is two measures in length with a repeat sign. The practice exercise chords last four measures each. By playing the sequence twice, you fill four measures.

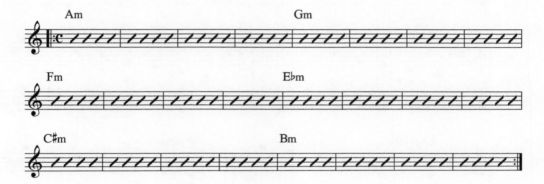

Playing Minor Arpeggios in Open Position

As a mandolin player, you need to become familiar (if not darned intimate) with all the minor arpeggios in open position. This position is important because it uses open strings, which makes certain musical passages a whole lot easier. The following figure shows the fingerings for all 12 minor arpeggios in open position.

When you've mastered these open-position minor arpeggios, apply them to the exercise on Track 86 using only open-position major arpeggios. Instead of moving the same pattern around the neck to match the chord changes, this time stay in one position playing nothing but open-position arpeggios.

Some but not all of the arpeggios contain open strings. With the open position, you play open strings when possible and don't go above the seventh fret for any notes.

Challenging Yourself: Minor Arpeggios on One String

This fun little exercise is merely the minor version of the one-string exercise I describe in Chapter 7, but this time it features four C minor one-string arpeggios:

1. **Begin with the G note at the open g-string.**

2. **Play the C note at the fifth fret of the g-string with your third finger.**

3. **Play the E♭ note at the eighth fret of the g-string with your first finger.**

4. **Play the G note at the 12th fret of the g-string with your third finger.**

5. **Play the arpeggio descending (down) using the same fingerings.** When you have the C minor arpeggio sounding clear on the g-string, move to the d-string and follow the same process.

Unlike the moveable arpeggio patterns of the earlier section 'Going To the Dark Side: Moveable Minor Arpeggios', one-string arpeggios don't have a consistent pattern when moving from string to string. Playing this type of arpeggio relies on your knowledge of the chord tones, not of shapes or patterns. Continue working on the same arpeggio on the a-string and the e-string.

The next figure which you can hear on Track 87 shows you a simple sequence for the C minor arpeggio for each of the four strings: (a) g-string; (b) d-string; (c) a-string; and (d) e-string.

You don't need to start on the root note, just the lowest possible chord tone of the string you're working on.

Track 87

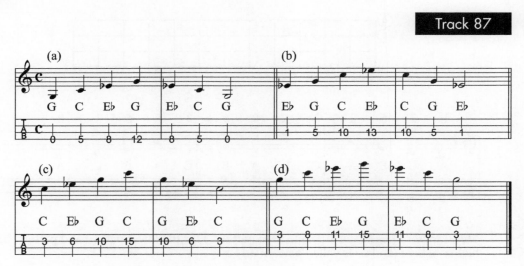

Practicing Minor Arpeggio Patterns over Two Octaves

The following two-octave G minor arpeggio uses open position for the first octave, followed by pattern 1. (For all four patterns in this section, see the earlier 'Going To the Dark Side: Moveable Minor Arpeggios' section.) This arpeggio requires a shift to *third position* (you usually play the fifth fret with the third finger, hence the term).

Check out the following figure for notation, tab, and a neck diagram for a simple sequence using the two-octave G minor arpeggio.

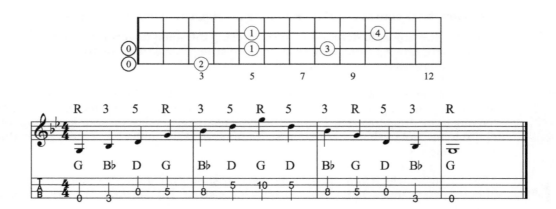

The following figure shows notation, tab, and a neck diagram for a simple sequence using the two-octave A minor arpeggio in open position.

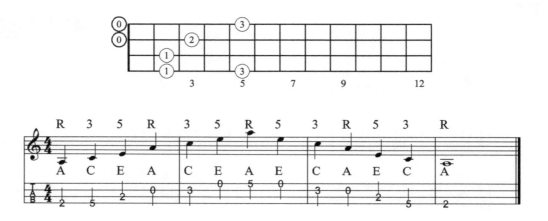

This C minor two-octave arpeggio uses pattern 3 for the lower octave and pattern 1 for the higher octave (and so is called pattern 3-1).

Make a small position shift at the octave to play this two-octave arpeggio. Instead of using your second finger for the octave, slide your hand up the neck a little and play the octave with your first finger. Now you're in position to play pattern 1 for the second octave of this two-octave arpeggio.

See the following figure for notation, tab, and a neck diagram for a simple sequence using the two-octave C minor arpeggio using pattern 3 followed by pattern 1.

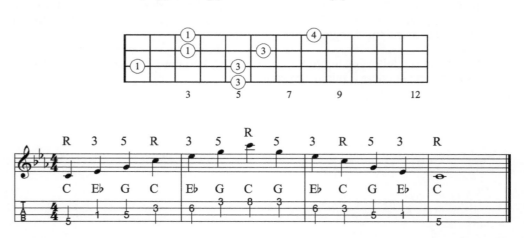

The pattern 2-1 for the two-octave arpeggio uses pattern 2 for the lower octave and pattern 1 for the higher octave. No position shift is needed to perform this two-octave arpeggio. Peruse the following figure for notation, tab, and a neck diagram for a simple sequence using the two-octave C minor arpeggio using pattern 2 and then pattern 1.

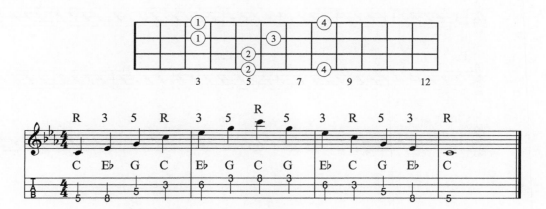

The pattern 1-1 two-octave arpeggio uses the same pattern for both octaves and requires a fairly large one finger position shift. In pattern 1, you play the root note with the first finger and the octave with the fourth finger. When playing the octave, move your left hand up the neck five frets and play the octave with the first finger, so setting yourself up nicely for the next pattern 1 arpeggio.

See the following figure for notation, tab, and a neck diagram for a simple sequence using the two-octave E minor arpeggio using pattern 1 followed by another pattern 1.

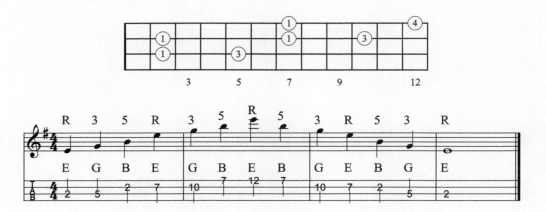

To test your two-octave minor arpeggio skills, practice playing the simple two-octave arpeggio sequence in this section, following the chord progression used in the following figure. You can use any combination of open position, moveable patterns, or one-string arpeggios. The important thing is that you're able to follow the chords and keep up with Track 88. Listen to this skankin' reggae track first to see how this exercise works, and then have a go at it.

The two-octave combinations I demonstrate also work with major arpeggios, and the combinations from Chapter 7 also work with minor arpeggios.

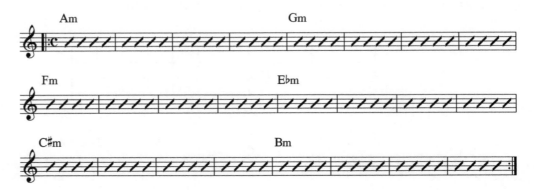

Chapter 9

Adding a Fourth Note to Create Seventh Arpeggios with Major Triads

In This Chapter
▶ Playing around with major seventh arpeggios
▶ Discovering dominant seventh arpeggios

Great things comes in threes, as the saying goes: Crosby, Stills, and Nash; The Three Stooges; Laurel and Hardy . . . no wait, something's wrong there! Anyway, you get the point.

As I describe in Chapter 7, an *arpeggio* is simply a chord played one note at a time. Plus a *triad* is just a fancy word for a three-note chord. In Chapters 7 and 8, I demonstrate basic major and minor chords (triads) that are made up of the *root* (name of the chord) and the *third* (the note that determines whether the chord is major or minor) and fifth degrees of a scale.

Well, seventh chords are simply triads with the seventh note of the scale added to them. (just as Crosby, Stills, and Nash were even better as Crosby, Stills, Nash, and Young, and nobody's ever heard of the Three Tops). For example, a triad contains three notes (the root, third, and fifth of a scale) and a seventh chord/arpeggio contains the root, third, fifth, and seventh notes of a scale. Seventh chords have a more colourful, complex sound than simple triads. This chapter explores two popular types of seventh arpeggios: major seventh (maj7) and dominant seventh arpeggios, which at their core are major triads.

Remembering the Seventies: Moveable Major Seventh Arpeggios

The major seventh chord was used occasionally throughout music history but became a defining element of the 1970s sound. Pop and rock groups such as Chicago, Bread, Blood Sweat, & Tears, America, and Led Zeppelin, as well as jazz artist Chick Corea and Brazilian bossa-nova composer Antônio Carlos Jobim, often used major seventh chords to convey that typical 1970s groovy feeling.

Major seventh chords/arpeggios are four-note chords made of the first, third, fifth, and seventh steps of a major scale. (Check out Chapter 3 for more on major scales.) For example, a C major seventh contains the notes C, E, G, and B. Notice that the first three notes in this chord are the C major triad (C, E, G). So the C major seventh chord is a C major triad plus the seventh note of the C major scale (B). The chord symbol for C major seventh is Cmaj7.

The following table shows the chord tones for each of the major seventh arpeggios.

Chord	Root	Third	Fifth	Seventh
Cmaj7	C	E	G	B
D♭maj7	D♭	F	A♭	C
Dmaj7	D	F#	A	C#
E♭maj7	E♭	G	B♭	D
Emaj7	E	G#	B	D#
Fmaj7	F	A	C	E
G♭maj7	G♭	B♭	D♭	F
Gmaj7	G	B	D	F#
A♭maj7	A♭	C	E♭	G
Amaj7	A	C#	E	G#
B♭maj7	B♭	D	F	A
Bmaj7	B	D#	F#	A#

Major seventh chords/arpeggios can be built on the *tonic* (first degree) of the major scale and the *sub-dominant* (fourth degree) of the major scale. Translation: Gmaj7 and Cmaj7 are the two possible major seventh chords in the key of G major.

In this section I show you four moveable major seventh arpeggio patterns and discuss playing major seventh arpeggios in open position, on one string, and over two octaves.

Major seventh arpeggio pattern 1

Major seventh arpeggio pattern 1 is derived from the major scale pattern 1 (see Chapter 3) and requires only two strings to play the complete arpeggio. This pattern is also similar to the major arpeggio pattern 1 in Chapter 7, with one additional note. This additional note is the seventh degree (note) in the major scale, hence the name major seventh.

Refer to the following figure for notation, tablature (tab), and a neck diagram for the Emaj7 arpeggio pattern 1. Listen to the example on Track 89 at www.dummies.com/go/mandolinexercises.

Track 89

Major seventh arpeggio pattern 2

I base major seventh arpeggio pattern 2 on the major scale pattern 2 (see Chapter 3); it requires three strings to play the complete arpeggio. This pattern is also similar to the major arpeggio pattern 2 in Chapter 7, with one additional note. This pattern starts with your second finger on the root note and finishes with your first finger on the octave.

This arpeggio pattern is quite a stretch, with two separate four-fret stretches (a major third interval) between your second and fourth fingers. If you find this difficult or even painful, check out some of the stretching and warm-up exercises in Chapter 2.

The following figure contains notation, tab, and a neck diagram for Gmaj7 arpeggio pattern 2, and Track 90 features an example.

Track 90

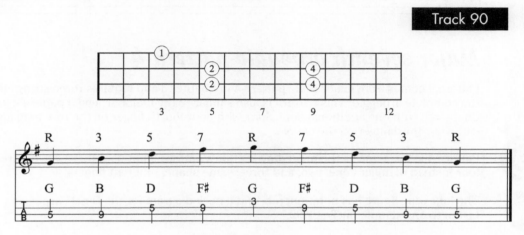

Some patterns or positions are easier to use simply because of finger strength, stretches and co-ordination issues than others. Although learning all the possibilities doesn't hurt you as a mandolin player, some patterns or positions are more common than others. Most people agree that shifting up the neck and playing the Gmaj7 arpeggio in pattern 1, or shifting down the neck and using Gmaj7 arpeggio pattern 3, is easier than playing the Gmaj7 arpeggio using pattern 2 (the one I just made you practice in the previous figure). When you experiment with a few possible positions, you discover that one sounds better or is easier to play than others – which is why you need to know all your possible options.

Major seventh arpeggio pattern 3

This pattern is derived from major scale pattern 3 (see Chapter 3) and requires three strings to play the complete arpeggio. This pattern is also similar to the major arpeggio pattern 3 in Chapter 7, with one additional note. You start with your third finger on the root note and finish with your second finger on the octave.

See the following figure for notation, tab, and a neck diagram for the Gmaj7 arpeggio pattern 3, and listen to Track 91.

Track 91

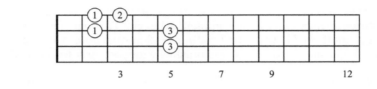

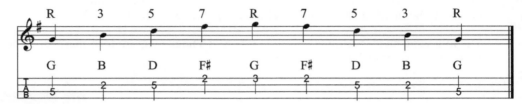

Major seventh arpeggio pattern 4

Pattern 4 comes from major scale pattern 4 in Chapter 3 and requires three strings to play the complete arpeggio. This pattern is also similar to the major arpeggio pattern 4 in Chapter 7, with one additional note. Start with your fourth finger on the root note and finish with your third finger on the octave.

Pattern 4 is the same as the preceding section's pattern 3 but uses fingers two, three, and four instead of fingers one, two, and three: same shape, different fingers.

The following figure has notation, tab, and a neck diagram for the Dmaj7 arpeggio pattern 4. Listen to an example on Track 92.

Track 92

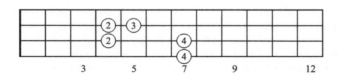

Slow dancing with major seventh arpeggios

Major seventh chords/arpeggios can have a romantic sound. The arpeggio sequence in the following figure (in 6/8 time) has been used in many love songs and shows the Amaj7 arpeggio using the four moveable patterns: (a) pattern 1, (b) pattern 2, (c) pattern 3, and (d) pattern 4. Let's call it 'Slow Dance Theme'.

Starting with pattern 1, memorize the simple sequence. Pick direction can be tricky in 6/8 time. For this sequence, use *jig picking,* (see *Mandolin For Dummies*) which is two sets of down–up–down strokes per measure.

Look closely at the following exercise and you can see that for this major seventh arpeggio sequence, patterns 1 and 2 use exactly the same frets, just different fingering. The same is true for patterns 3 and 4 in this exercise. By developing a variety of ways to play the same thing, you expand your musical possibilities and so become a better mandolin player.

This exercise tests your knowledge of the fingerboard by requiring you to apply the moveable major seventh arpeggio sequence from the preceding figure 'Slow Dance Theme' to a chord progression (a series of chords). Be sure to listen to Track 93 which is slightly reminiscent of the band Chicago's early 1970's slow dance favorite 'Colour My World' to see how this exercise works:

1. **Work through the entire chord progression using only pattern 1, until you can get through the practice track with this pattern.**

2. **Memorize 'Slow Dance Theme' using patterns 2, 3, and 4.**

3. **Go through the exercise focusing on one pattern at a time until you can get through the entire exercise using each of the four patterns.**

If it feels like the 1970s, you're getting the hang of it!

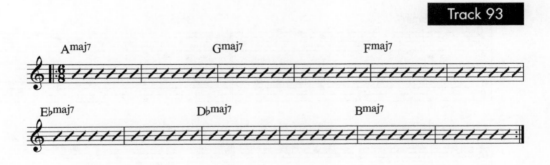

Be sure to download all the audio tracks for this book at www.dummies.com/go/ mandolinexercises. Hearing the examples is a sure way to know whether you're playing them correctly. In all the arpeggio and scale exercise tracks, I play the exercise along with the backing track the first time through. The second time, I drop out and leave it up to you.

Groovin' with major seventh arpeggios in open position

As with scales, mandolin players need to be familiar with all major seventh arpeggios in open position (which is important because open position uses open strings, so making certain musical passages easier). The downside of playing in open position is that each arpeggio or scale has its own unique pattern or shape on the fingerboard. The following figure shows all 12 major seventh arpeggios in open position.

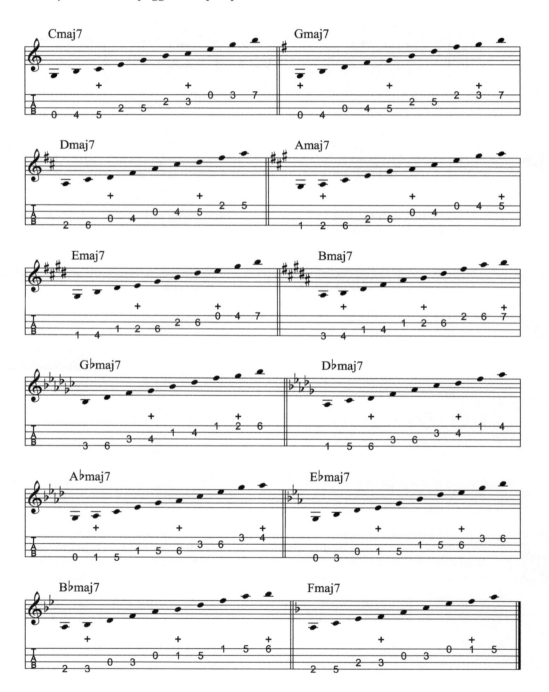

When you have these open-position major seventh arpeggios under your fingers, try the next exercise, bearing in mind the following simple rules:

✔ **Stay in open position using open strings whenever possible.**

✔ **Follow the chord progression using only chord tones.**

✔ **Follow the chord progression using only quarter notes (crotchets).**

✔ **Use good voice leading when transitioning from one chord to another.**

Voice leading is a technique that arrangers use to create a smooth transition from chord to chord by moving each individual note the smallest interval or distance possible. This exercise uses a form of melodic voice leading to connect one chord to another.

I place brackets over the transition notes that demonstrate good voice leading. Listen to Track 94 and see the following figure for a demonstration of this exercise. The second time through, I stop playing and let you get into the driver's seat and play whatever notes you want, as long as you follow the rules. Don't just memorize what I play.

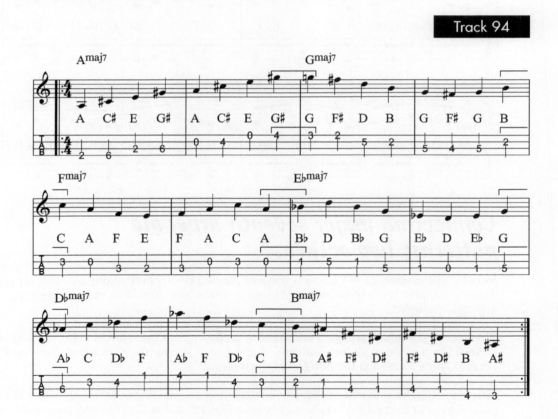

Playing with the higher frets: Major seventh arpeggios on one string

By deliberately restricting yourself with practice exercises that limit the use of certain fingers, strings, or certain pick direction, you will become a better mandolin player. By forcing you outside of your comfort zone, you will see the mandolin in a different light, allowing you to see things that you were unable to see before.

The following figure demonstrates the same six major seventh chords/arpeggios I use earlier in this chapter (in the section 'Groovin with major seventh arpeggios in open position'), but this time they're all on the g-string. Notice that each arpeggio starts on the lowest possible chord tone on the g-string, not necessarily the root note of the chord. To reach enlightenment on the mandolin, you need to learn to play all types of arpeggios on each string.

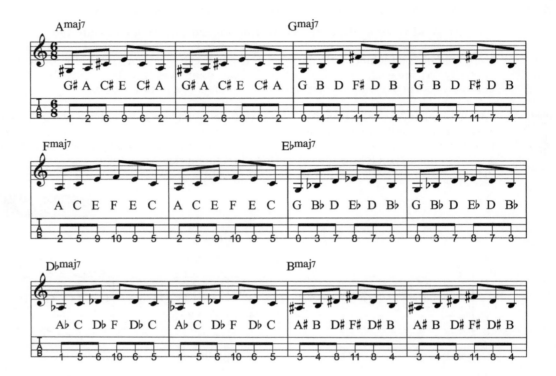

Connecting major seventh arpeggio patterns: Two octaves

Here I demonstrate a few common ways of playing two-octave major seventh arpeggios. These examples include elements of open position and moveable major seventh arpeggio patterns.

The two-octave Gmaj7 arpeggio in the following figure uses open position for the first octave, followed by a position shift to pattern 1 that requires you to place your first finger on the octave G note located at the fifth fret of the d-string.

This transition from fourth-fret F♯, played with your second finger, followed by the fifth fret played by your first finger, may seem like an awkward shift at first but becomes easier with practice. This type of two finger shift is covered in Chapter 6.

The figure shows notation, tab, and a neck diagram for the two-octave Gmaj7 arpeggio pattern 0-1.

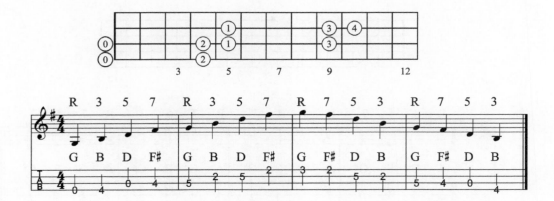

The next two-octave Amaj7 arpeggio uses pattern 1 for the lower octave and open position for the second octave.

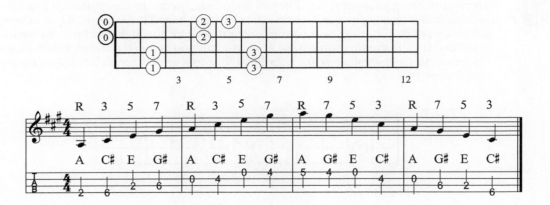

The pattern 1-3 two-octave Amaj7 arpeggio uses pattern 1 for the lower octave and pattern 3 for the higher octave.

You have to make a small position shift to play this two-octave arpeggio. Notice that for Amaj7 pattern 1 (see 'Remembering the Seventies: Moveable Major Seventh Arpeggios'), your third finger plays the seventh or the G# note of the Amaj7 arpeggio, which is located at the sixth fret of the d string, which is followed by your fourth finger playing the octave. Instead of using your fourth finger for the octave, slide or shift your third finger from the G# to the octave A, or from the sixth fret to the seventh fret. Now you're in position to play pattern 3 for the second octave of this two-octave arpeggio. Use the same slide or shift when descending.

See the following figure for notation, tab, and a neck diagram for the two-octave Amaj7 arpeggio using pattern 1-3.

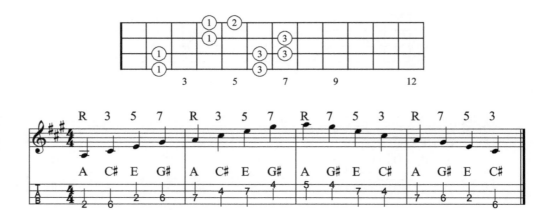

You can connect arpeggios in more than one way. Depending on the piece of music and your physical limitations, one method may be easier for you than another. Good practice involves pushing yourself to try different fingerings, but in the end you want to make the most beautiful music you can by using the skills you have. The pattern 1-4 two-octave arpeggio uses pattern 1 for the lower octave and pattern 4 for the higher octave. No position shift is needed to perform this two-octave arpeggio, but you do need a strong fourth finger. Check out the following figure for notation, tab, and a neck diagram for this two octave Amaj7 arpeggio.

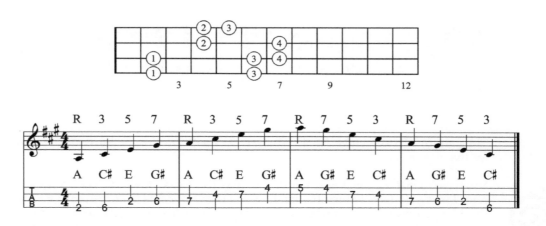

The following arpeggio sequence uses two-octave major seventh arpeggios, following a similar chord progression to that which I present earlier in this chapter (in 'Slow dancing with major seventh arpeggios'). Notice that this sequence doesn't require the full two octaves, but more like one and a half octaves. Play this sequence using only down-strokes.

Work on recognizing the patterns in this exercise. I use brackets below the tablature to illustrate the use of different patterns. I also place finger numbers above the tab to make the patterns and shifts easier to see and understand.

This sequence doesn't use key signatures to determine the sharps or flats, but *accidentals* (which are sharp, flat, or natural signs directly before the note on the musical staff). Try to become comfortable with both types of notation.

Track 95 finds you grooving to a jazzy bossa nova beat (you remember 'The Girl From Ipanema' don't you?). The track plays through this exercise twice so follow along with me the first time through and then take it on your own with the band the second time. Have fun!

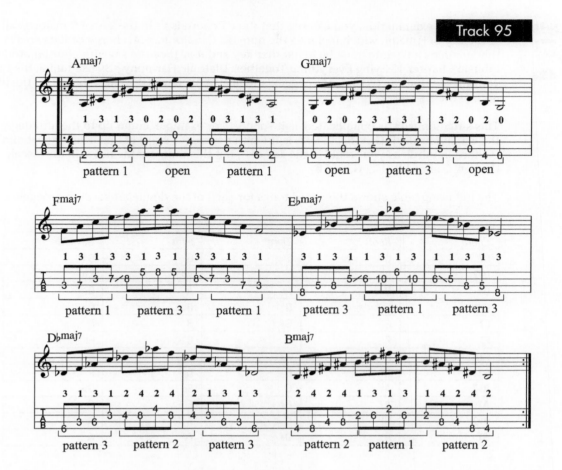

Dominating your Mandolin with Moveable Dominant Seventh Arpeggios

Dominant seventh chords and arpeggios are a little unsettled and can create the feeling of unresolve or movement. Dominant seventh chords are used in many musical styles including folk, country, blues, jazz, funk, choro, classical and probably even more. The dominant seventh chord is built on the fifth degree of major scales (see Chapter 3) and the harmonic minor scales (see Chapter 4). Blues musicians rely heavily on this dominant seventh sound, maybe due to it's unresolved nature. Rhythm and blues musicians can pack the dance floor using one or two dominant seventh chords with an infectiously funky groove.

The dominant seventh is indicated in chord symbols simply by placing a 7 immediately after the chord name. For example, the chord symbol for a C dominant seventh chord is simply C7. Dominant seventh chords consist of the root, third, and fifth degrees of the scale, but the seventh is altered or flatted by one half step (one fret). C major contains the notes C, E, and G, and therefore C7 contains C, E, G, and B♭. As I reveal in the earlier section 'Remembering the Seventies: Moveable Major Seventh Arpeggios', Cmaj7 contains the notes C, E, G, and B, and so the only difference in the dominant seventh is that the seventh note is flatted (played one fret lower).

Upon close examination, you can see that the C7 chord isn't in the key of C major at all but in the key of F major, which includes the note B♭. C major has no sharps or flats so a chord that contains a B♭ note must be in another key and it is! (See the seventh chord diatonic table in Chapter 12 Tying Everything Together: Diatonic Harmony.) By examining the table you will see that the C7 chord/arpeggio is really the V chord (the chord based on the fifth note of the F scale).

This situation isn't as complicated as it sounds. For example, count up to the fifth degree of the F major scale: F, G, A, B♭, C. So C is the fifth degree (or step) of that scale. Now build the C chord in thirds as you would in the key of C, but this time use the notes in the F scale. So the new C chord is C, E, G, and B♭.

The following table shows the chord tones for each of the dominant seventh arpeggios.

Chord	Root	Third	Fifth	Seventh
C7	C	E	G	B♭
D♭7	D♭	F	A♭	C♭
D7	D	F#	A	C
E♭7	E♭	G	B♭	D♭
E7	E	G#	B	D
F7	F	A	C	E♭
F#7	F#	A#	C#	E
G7	G	B	D	F
A♭7	A♭	C	E♭	G♭
A7	A	C#	E	G
B♭7	B♭	D	F	A♭
B7	B	D#	F#	A

Dominant seventh chords/arpeggios are built on the fifth degree of major and harmonic minor scales. So D7 isn't in the key of D, but G major or possibly G minor. For this reason I present all dominant seventh arpeggios in the proper major key, and so D7 has the key signature of one sharp of G major.

In this section I show you four moveable dominant seventh arpeggio patterns and discuss playing dominant seventh arpeggios in open position, on one string, and over two octaves.

Dominant seventh arpeggio pattern 1

Dominant seventh arpeggio pattern 1 is very similar to the major arpeggio pattern 1 from Chapter 7, with one additional note: the flatted seventh degree (or note) in the major scale.

Look over the following figure for notation, tab, and a neck diagram for the E7 arpeggio pattern 1, and listen to the example on Track 96.

Track 96

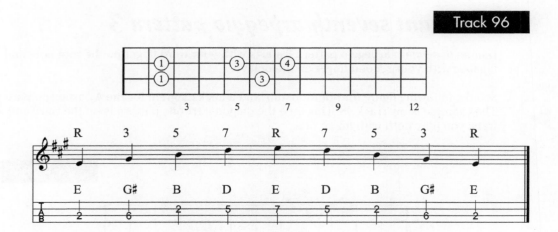

 Dominant seventh arpeggios contain an interesting and fairly dissonant interval known as a *tritone*. A tritone interval (sometimes called a diminished fifth or even an augmented fourth) is the distance of six frets (or four whole steps), which turns out to be exactly one half of an octave. Tritones form a diagonal pattern on the mandolin fingerboard (fourth fret d-string, third fret a-string, and so on) and are present in many of the more exotic chords/arpeggios. Try to spot the tritone in each of the dominant seventh arpeggio patterns.

Dominant seventh arpeggio pattern 2

 To play the dominant seventh arpeggio pattern 2, start with your second finger on the root note and finish with your first finger on the octave.

The following figure contains notation, tab, and a neck diagram for the G7 arpeggio pattern 2. Listen to the example on Track 97.

 Spot the diagonal tritone pattern at the ninth and eighth frets.

Track 97

Dominant seventh arpeggio pattern 3

Dominant seventh arpeggio pattern 3 starts with your third finger on the root note and finishes with your second finger on the octave.

See the following figure for notation, tab, and a neck diagram for the A7 arpeggio pattern 3. The example is on Track 98. This time the diagonal tritone pattern is on the third and fourth frets; you play both with finger one.

Track 98

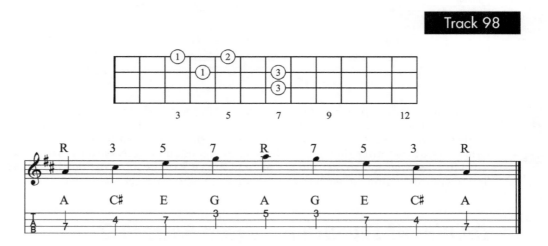

Dominant seventh arpeggio pattern 4

Dominant seventh arpeggio pattern 4 requires you to use your fourth finger on the root note and finish with your third finger on the octave.

As I discuss in Chapter 7, pattern 4 is the same as pattern 3, but instead of using fingers one, two, and three, you use fingers two, three, and four: same shape, different fingers.

Check out the following figure for notation, tab, and a neck diagram for the D7 arpeggio pattern 4, and turn your ears to the example on Track 99.

Track 99

Rockin' out with a dominant seventh riff

Dominant seventh chords/arpeggios often produce a bluesy or early rock-n-roll type of sound. In fact the following sequence could easily be called a riff. The term sequence seems a bit too stuffy for this type of sound so feel free to let down your hair a little and have a little fun with this moveable dominant seventh riff.

The following figure shows the A7 riff using the four moveable patterns: (a) pattern 1, (b) pattern 2, (c) pattern 3, (d) pattern 4. Starting with pattern 1, memorize the riff in all four patterns. Left hand fingerings are placed above the tablature.

Notice that patterns 1 and 2 are the same notes, located at the same frets but played with different fingering. Most people agree that pattern 1 is easier, but depending on the melody or riff and also depending on what key you are playing in you might find that pattern 2 works better.

Try to follow the chord progression in the following figure by playing the appropriate moveable dominant seventh *riff* to match the chords. Be sure to listen to the blues shuffle rhythm section on Track 100 to see how this exercise works. Play the riff using pattern 1 for all six of the chords. When you can get through the entire practice track using pattern 1, go back and memorize the same sequence using patterns 2, 3, and 4. Next go through the exercise focusing on one pattern at a time until you can get through the entire exercise. Then give yourself a high-five if nobody's looking.

Track 100

Staying put with dominant seventh arpeggios in open position

As when playing scales, mandolin players need to become familiar with all arpeggios in open position. Open position uses open strings and makes certain musical passages much easier.

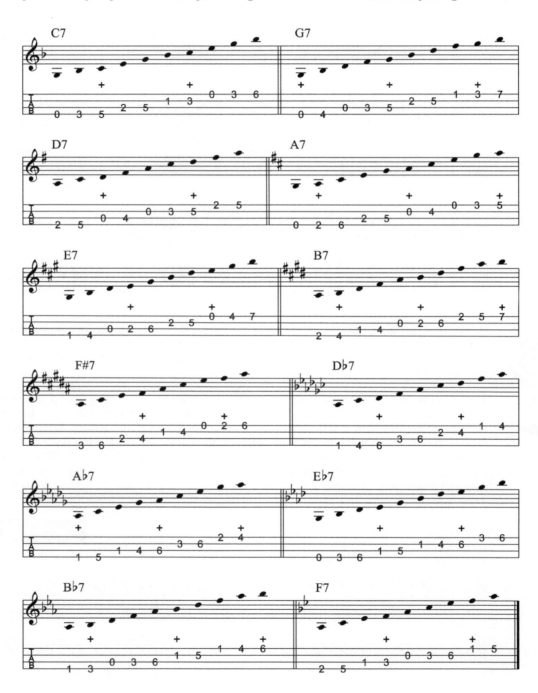

When you feel comfortable with these open-position dominant seventh arpeggios, try the following exercise. Bear in mind the four rules I identify in the earlier section 'Groovin' with major seventh arpeggios in open position'.

Listen to Track 101 and see the following figure for a demonstration of this exercise. Remember that the second time through, I stop playing and leave it up to you. You then have a chance to play whatever you want, as long as it follows the rules. Basically chord tones, quarter, notes, stay in position, voice leading. Don't just memorize what I play.

Uncovering dominant seventh arpeggios on one string

The following figure demonstrates how to play six dominant seventh chords/arpeggios without ever leaving the d-string!

Each arpeggio starts on the lowest possible chord tone on the d-string, not necessarily the root note of the chord.

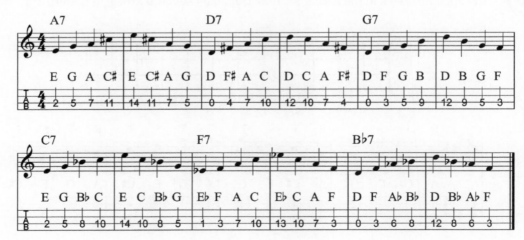

Connecting dominant seventh arpeggio patterns: Two octaves

I now demonstrate a few common ways of playing two-octave dominant seventh arpeggios. The examples include elements of open position and moveable dominant seventh arpeggio patterns.

The following two-octave G dominant seventh arpeggio uses open position for the first octave, followed by a shift to dominant seventh pattern 1 in third position, requiring you to place your first finger on the fifth fret of the d-string. You usually play the fifth fret with the third finger, hence the term *third position*.

The following figure has notation, tab, and a neck diagram for the two-octave G7 arpeggio 0-1.

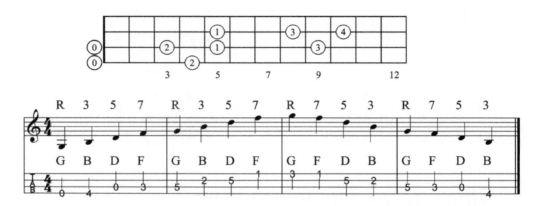

The two-octave A7 1-0 arpeggio shown next stays in open position for both octaves. Even though you're in open position, you're still using pattern 1 for the lower octave. Instead of finishing the lower octave on fret seven of the d-string, play the open a-string and continue the arpeggio using open strings whenever possible.

Notice how in this pattern, the diagonal tritone pattern stretches across all four pairs of strings, starting at the sixth fret of the g-string and ending at the third fret of the e-string. (I explain tritones in the earlier section 'Dominant seventh arpeggio pattern 1'.)

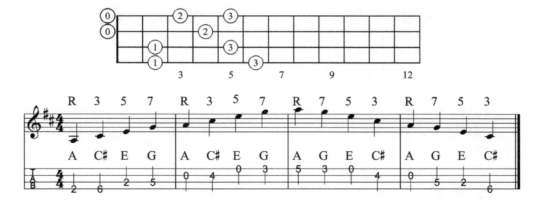

The pattern 1-3 two-octave dominant seventh arpeggio uses pattern 1 for the lower octave and pattern 3 for the higher octave.

You need to make a small position shift to play this two-octave arpeggio. The shift happens at the octave. Instead of using your fourth finger for the octave, which would be standard in pattern 1, slide or shift your ring finger that's on the seventh of the chord up two frets to the octave. Now you're in position to play pattern 3 for the second octave of this two-octave arpeggio.

See the following figure for notation, tab, and a neck diagram for the two-octave A7 arpeggio pattern 1-3.

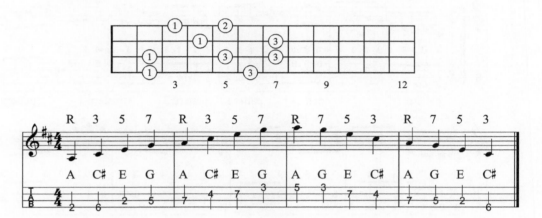

The pattern 1-4 two-octave arpeggio uses pattern 1 for the lower octave and pattern 4 for the higher octave. No position shift is needed to perform this two-octave arpeggio, but you need a strong fourth finger. See the following figure for notation, tab, and a neck diagram for this pattern.

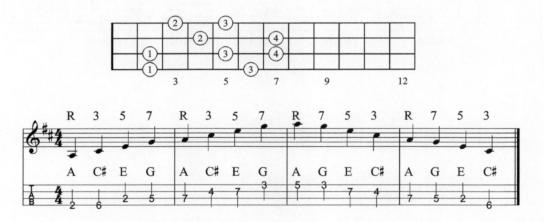

The following workout uses two-octave dominant seventh arpeggios, but not the full two octaves – it's more like one and a half. Watch out for all the slides. I suggest playing this using only down-strokes.

Recognizing the patterns in this exercise is vitally important. I employ brackets below the tablature to illustrate the different patterns. I also place finger numbers above the tab to make the patterns and shifts easier to see and understand.

The exercise uses a *blue note:* a note that's not part of the arpeggio or even the key that the arpeggio is built from. This blue note is the flatted third of the chord. Normally the flatted third indicates a minor chord/arpeggio, but in this case it's used to add a bluesy quality to the dominant seventh arpeggio sequence.

Track 102 has you sitting in with a cool jazz quartet. Lucky for you, these cats take it easy on you by playing this arpeggio workout at a relaxed (medium slow) tempo. Follow along with me the first time through and then you are on your own.

Track 102

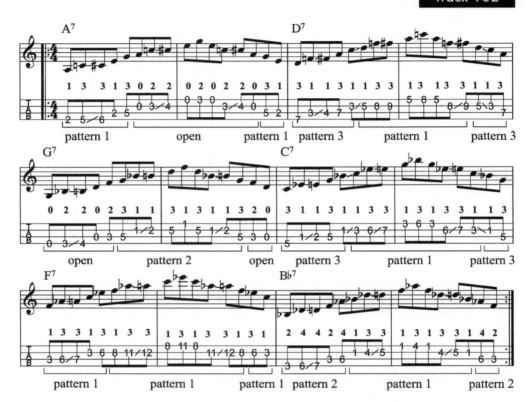

Chapter 10

Summoning up Seventh Arpeggios of the Minor Variety

*I*f you're drawn to the dark side and like scary movies, hanging out in graveyards at midnight, or Black Sabbath, you may one day ask yourself, 'What happens if I add a seventh note to a minor chord? What mysterious forces does that summon up?'. Well wonder no more. Minor sevenths are still minor chords but with a level of sophistication. In fact minor seventh chords are often found in major keys. More on this in the next section. These chords have been a staple in jazz since the 1940s but can also be found in pop music for grown-ups (sometimes called soft rock) in the music of Steely Dan, James Taylor, Carole King, Fleetwood Mac, Sting. Minor seven flat five chords on the other hand can have a downright depressed or even sinister sound. Think of a slow jazz ballad with mournful tenor sax in a smokey after hour club. Dark and sophisticated.

In this chapter I explore two types of seventh arpeggios: the jazzy minor seventh (m7) and dissonant and even esoteric minor seven flat five (m7♭5).

Feeling Jazzy: Moveable Minor Seventh Arpeggios

The minor seventh chord/arpeggio has a smooth and somewhat refined sound and is a staple in jazz-style chord progressions. Duke Ellington, Cole Porter, Hoagy Carmichael, George Gershwin, and many other wonderful jazz composers use minor seventh and other complex chords to great effect. In the mandolin world, you can hear the minor seventh chords/arpeggios I present in this chapter (and indeed the dominant and major sevenths in Chapter 9) in the jazzier music of David Grisman, Don Stiernberg, Paul Glasse, Will Patton, and many of the Brazilian choro mandolin players including Dudu Maia, Jacob do Bandolim, and Hamilton De Holanda.

You won't be surprised to discover that minor seventh chords/arpeggios are four-note chords comprising the first, third, fifth, and seventh steps of the natural minor scale (see Chapter 4 for more). But they can also be constructed from major scales. (You may want to reread that again and let it sink in.) Yes, that's right: you can construct a minor seventh chord starting on the second degree of a major scale. For example, an Am7 chord can be made up of notes from the G major scale, starting at the second note of the scale. So by using the second, fourth, sixth, and eighth notes of the G major scale, you arrive at A, C, E, and G, which ends up being the chord tones for an Am7 chord. This relationship of a minor seventh chord to the second note of a scale is a crucial part of jazz harmony.

The following table shows the chord tones for each of the 12 minor seventh arpeggios.

Chord	Root	Third	Fifth	Seventh
Cm7	C	E♭	G	B♭
C#m7	C#	E	G#	B
Dm7	D	F	A	C
E♭m7	E♭	G♭	B♭	D♭
Em7	E	G	B	D
Fm7	F	A♭	C	E♭
F#m7	F#	A	C#	E
Gm7	G	B♭	D	F
G#m7	G#	B	D#	F#
Am7	A	C	E	G
B♭m7	B♭	D♭	F	A♭
Bm7	B	D	F#	A

Minor seventh chords/arpeggios are built on the second, third, and sixth degrees of the major scale. Translation: Am7, Bm7, and Em7 are the three possible diatonic minor seventh chords in the key of G major.

Look at these arpeggio patterns as geometric shapes, because they then become easier to remember and use to make up melodies if you're the improvising type. Notice (in the next two sections) the shape of a rectangular box in pattern 1 and pattern 2, which consists of two notes played three frets apart (a minor third apart) on adjacent strings.

Minor seventh arpeggio pattern 1

Minor seventh arpeggio pattern 1 is very similar to the minor arpeggio pattern 1 in Chapter 8, with one additional note.

See the following figure for notation, tablature (tab), and a neck diagram for the Em7 arpeggio pattern 1, and listen to the example on Track 103 www.dummies.com/go/mandolinexercises.

Track 103

Even though I demonstrate every arpeggio in four closed positions, patterns 1 and 3 are more common than patterns 2 and 4, because the latter two patterns rely more on your fourth finger. No matter how much you practice, your fourth finger is never going to be as strong as fingers one, two, and three.

Minor seventh arpeggio pattern 2

Pattern 2 starts with your second finger on the root note and finishes with your first finger on the octave.

Check out the following figure for notation, tab, and a neck diagram for the Gm7 arpeggio pattern 2. I play an example on Track 104.

Track 104

The four moveable minor seventh arpeggio patterns are very similar to the four moveable minor arpeggio patterns in Chapter 8. The minor seventh arpeggios contain the first, third, fifth, and seventh steps of the natural minor scale, while maintaining the same basic hand position or pattern.

Minor seventh arpeggio pattern 3

Start pattern 3 with your third finger on the root note and finish with your second finger on the octave.

The following figure has notation, tab, and a neck diagram for the Am7 arpeggio pattern 3. Listen to an example on Track 105.

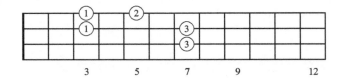

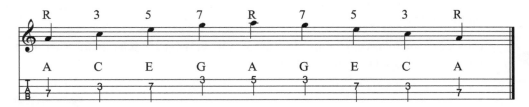

Minor seventh arpeggio pattern 4

TIP

PLAY THIS!

Pattern 4 starts with your fourth finger on the root note and finishes with your third finger on the octave.

As you can see in Chapter 7, pattern 4 is the same as pattern 3, but instead of using fingers one, two, and three, you use fingers two, three, and four: same shape, different fingers.

The following figure contains notation, tab, and a neck diagram for the Dm7 arpeggio pattern 4, and Track 106 has the example.

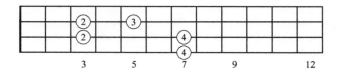

Messing with minor seventh arpeggio patterns

If your tastes tend to lean toward the cosmopolitan side of the spectrum and you enjoy wine tasting events, art openings and jazz concerts, minor seventh chords and arpeggios might be just the ticket for you. Sophisticated and intellectual without being exclusive or super rich.

The following figure shows an easy Am7 lick using the four moveable patterns: (a) pattern 1, (b) pattern 2, (c) pattern 3, and (d) pattern 4. Starting with pattern 1, memorize the lick in all four patterns shown in the figure, playing it using all down-strokes.

One of the biggest advantages of becoming proficient with the four moveable patterns turns out to be the opposite of what you may think. Instead of jumping all over the fingerboard using the same pattern to follow a chord progression, you're able to stay in one region and use a variety of patterns. For example: start the exercise by playing the Am7 lick using pattern 3, with your third finger on the seventh fret of the d-string. For Em7, use pattern 4, which starts with your fourth finger on the ninth fret of the g-string. For Dm7, use pattern 3 by placing your third finger on the seventh fret of the g-string. Your left hand stays in position while you play the lick over three different chords.

Good luck with the following exercise, demonstrated with a medium slow tempo Afro-Cuban rhythm style called a bolero on Track 107.

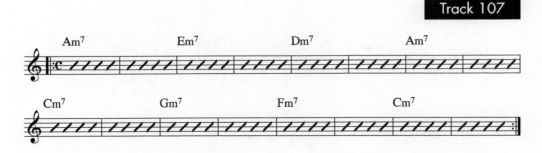

When you're sure that you understand this or any of the exercises in this book, feel free to practice them in as many keys as you can. Push yourself: the goal is to be able to play any lick or exercise in any key.

Focusing on minor seventh arpeggios in open position

You need to become familiar with all minor seventh arpeggios in open position, because open strings make playing certain musical passages much easier. Unfortunately, however, in open position each arpeggio or scale has its own unique pattern or shape on the fingerboard.

The following figure shows all 12 major arpeggios in open position.

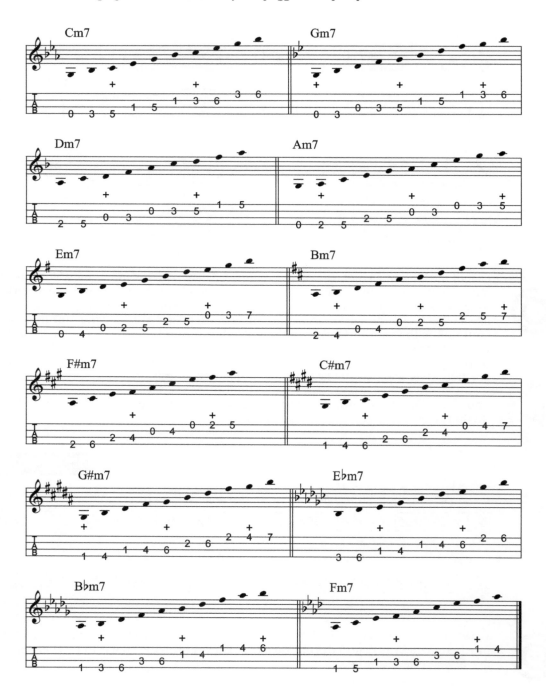

Practice these open-position minor seventh arpeggios. When you're confident, try out the following exercise, bearing in mind these simple rules:

✔ **Stay in open position using open strings whenever possible.**

✔ **Follow the chord progression using only chord tones.**

✔ **Follow the chord progression using only quarter notes (crotchets).**

✔ **Use good voice leading (which I explain in Chapter 9) when transitioning from one chord to another.**

I position brackets over the transition notes that demonstrate good voice leading. Listen to Track 108 and see the following figure for a demonstration of this exercise. I stop playing the second time through and leave you to solo.

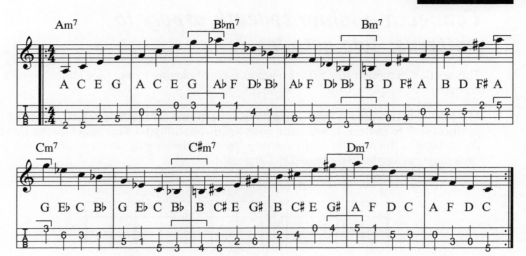

Track 108

Revealing minor seventh arpeggios on one string

The following figure demonstrates four minor seventh chords/arpeggios (Am7, Cm7, E♭m7, F♯m7) on the a-string only. I include note names above the tab so that you can verify that these are indeed chord tones.

At first, feel free to follow the tab, but when you truly understand this one-string arpeggio concept you should be able to play this exercise using the chord symbols only. Notice that each arpeggio starts on the lowest possible chord tone on the a-string, not necessarily the root note of the chord.

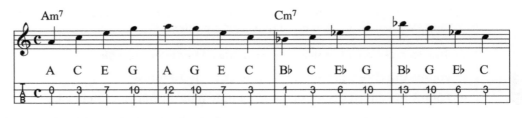

Connecting minor seventh arpeggio patterns: Two octaves

This section demonstrates a few common ways of playing two-octave minor seventh arpeggios.

The following two-octave Dm7 arpeggio uses pattern 3 for the first octave, followed by a position shift to pattern 1, requiring you to slide or shift your first finger on the third fret of the a-string to the fifth fret of the a-string. See the following figure for notation, tab, and a neck diagram for the two-octave Dm7 arpeggio 3-1.

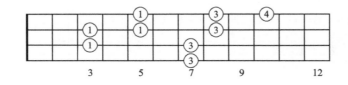

The next two-octave Dm7 arpeggio uses pattern 3 for the lower octave and pattern 2 for the second octave.

This 3-2 two-octave pattern uses the same notes played at the same frets with a slightly different fingering than for the two-octave pattern 3-1. Another case of same sound, different fingering patterns – one that requires you to make a position shift and one that requires you to use your fourth finger.

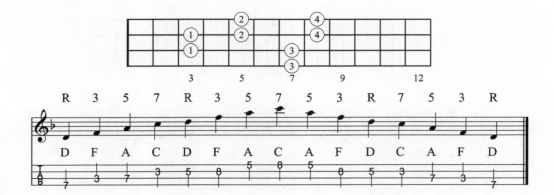

The pattern 2-1 two-octave Cm7 arpeggio uses pattern 2 for the lower octave and pattern 1 for the higher octave. No position shift is required to play this two-octave arpeggio, allowing you to stay in position (phew!). See the following figure for notation, tab, and a neck diagram for the two-octave Cm7 arpeggio pattern 2-1.

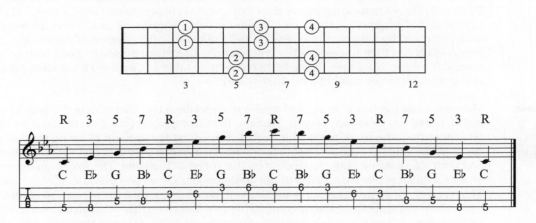

The pattern 1-1 two-octave Cm7 arpeggio uses pattern 1 for the lower octave and pattern 1 again for the higher octave. This two-octave pattern requires you to shift down two frets from the fifth fret to the third fret for the second octave.

Notice the rectangular box pattern on the g- and d-strings between the fifth and eighth frets and then again on the a- and e-strings between the third and seventh frets.

Use the following figure for notation, tab, and a neck diagram for the two-octave Cm7 arpeggio pattern 1-1.

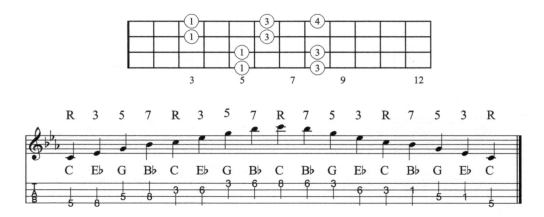

Progressing to some jazzy phrases

The ii/V7/I chord progression (pronounced two–five–one) and its unresolved sibling, the ii/V7 chord progressions are some of the most common progressions in jazz music of the 1940s to 1970s. This progression starts with a minor seventh chord built on the second degree of the scale, followed by a dominant seventh chord built on the fifth degree of the same scale. The progression can then be resolved or completed with a major seventh chord built on the first note of the same scale (see the seventh chord tone table in Chapter 12). So this progression in the key of G major would be Am7/D7/Gmaj7.

Musicians use the terms *swing* and *shuffle* to describe a feel that affects the way in which eighth notes (quavers) are played. Think of the strong beats (numbered beats) as being a bit longer than the weak beats (the 'ands'). You adjust the amount of swing by making the down-beats longer, resulting in shorter up-beats. You can play this feel with all down-strokes and with alternate picking, depending on the speed of the song. The following figure demonstrates a musical phrase applied to the common jazz chord progression ii/V7 (two-five). This type of chord progression is unresolved, leaving you with the sensation of motion or the feeling that something else is going to happen. Compare this unresolved chord progression to a resolved minor key version of this same type of progression in Swinging with a jazzy minor seven flat five sequence. If you were comparing it to punctuation used in writing, the ii/V7/ would seem like a place for a comma, while the ii/V7/I would seem more like a good place for a period.

The sequence (or musical phrase) is demonstrated in six different keys using a variety of arpeggio patterns.

This phrase doesn't require the full two octaves, but more like one and a half. Make the effort to recognize the patterns used in this exercise. To help, I place brackets below the tab to illustrate the use of different patterns. I also print finger numbers above the tab to make the patterns and shifts easier.

Play this jazzy phrase in a swing style using only down-strokes. You can hear it on Track 109.

What's in a name?

Naming chords can get pretty esoteric when you get beyond the basic triads. For example, if you take the chord Am7, which contains the notes A, C, E, and G, and compare it to the chord C6, which contains the notes C, E, G, and A, you can see that they're the same notes in a different order. The same thing happens with Am7♭5, which includes A, C, E♭, and G, compared with Cm6, which is made up of C, E♭, G, and A. This is another good case for memorizing the names of the notes in each arpeggio.

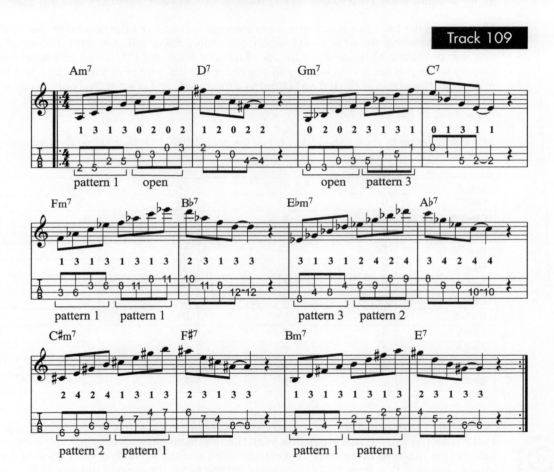

Practicing Moveable Minor Seven Flat Five Arpeggios

The seventh chord/arpeggio I discuss in this section is the minor seven flat five (m7♭5; sometimes called half-diminished). Therefore, for example, the chord symbol for C minor seventh flat five is Cm7♭5.

Minor seven flat five chords/arpeggios have a dark, complex sound that are an essential sound of jazz of the 1930s through the 1960s. Minor seven flat five arpeggios or chords are found primarily in minor key songs which by nature have a darker sound than major key songs. Some minor key songs from that era that use these chords/arpeggios that have become jazz standards would include 'After Midnight', 'Alone Together', 'Beautiful Love', 'What Is This Thing Called Love', 'You Don't Know What Love Is'.

Don't let the m7♭5 name scare you, because this chord/arpeggio is constructed from major and minor scales just like the rest of the chords/arpeggios in this book. The *triad* (the primary three notes) of this chord form a diminished chord, which contains a root note, a flatted third (like all minor chords), and a flatted fifth. The m7♭5 also includes the flatted or minor seventh note. Turn to Chapter 11 for more about diminished seventh arpeggios.

Minor seven flat five chords/arpeggios are commonly built from the second degree of the natural or harmonic minor scales (Chapter 4 has more about minor scales). Technically they can also be built from the seventh degree of a major scale, but this isn't a common chord. Usually when you see m7♭5 chords you can recognize that you're in a minor key, and the m7♭5 chord/arpeggio is the ii (two) chord in a minor key and is most likely followed by a V7 (five) chord in the same key. For example, Bm7♭5 followed by E7 is considered a minor ii/V7 in the key of Am.

The following table shows the chord tones for each of the 12 minor seven flat five arpeggios.

Chord	Root	Third	Fifth	Seventh
Cm7♭5	C	E♭	G♭	B♭
C#m7♭5	C#	E	G	B
Dm7♭5	D	F	A♭	C
D#m7♭5	D#	F#	A	C#
Em7♭5	E	G	B♭	D
Fm7♭5	F	A♭	C♭	E♭
F#m7♭5	F#	A	C	E
Gm7♭5	G	B♭	D♭	F
G#m7♭5	G#	B	D	F#
Am7♭5	A	C	E♭	G
Bbm7♭5	B♭	D♭	F♭	A♭
Bm7♭5	B	D	F	A

Notice that the diagonal tritone pattern (which I define for you in Chapter 9) is also present in the minor seven flat five arpeggios. With the dominant seventh arpeggios, the tritone interval (or diagonal pattern) is between the third and the seventh of the chord. In the minor seven flat five arpeggio, the diagonal tritone pattern connects the root note with the altered or flatted fifth.

Minor seven flat five arpeggio pattern 1

Minor seven flat five arpeggio pattern 1 starts with your first finger and finishes with your fourth finger. This pattern 1 is very similar to pattern 1 in the earlier section 'Minor seventh arpeggio pattern 1', with one altered note: the flatted fifth.

Check out the following figure for notation, tab, and a neck diagram for the Em7♭5 arpeggio pattern 1, and listen to the example on Track 110.

Track 110

These chords are built on the second degree of a minor scale. For this reason I choose to present all minor seven flat five arpeggios in the proper key, and so Em7♭5 has the key signature of one flat or D minor.

Minor seven flat five arpeggio pattern 2

Start minor seven flat five arpeggio pattern 2 with your second finger on the root note and finish with your first finger on the octave. Notice the diagonal tritone pattern on the fingerboard at frets five, four, and three.

The following figure contains notation, tab, and a neck diagram for the Gm7♭5 arpeggio pattern 2. Listen to the example on Track 111.

Track 111

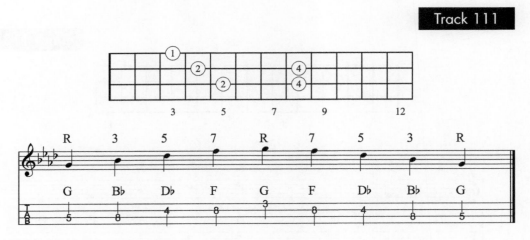

Minor seven flat five arpeggio pattern 3

Minor seven flat five arpeggio pattern three starts with your third finger on the root note and finishes with your second finger on the octave. The diagonal tritone pattern is on the fingerboard at frets seven, six, and five.

See the following figure for notation, tab, and a neck diagram for the Am7♭5 arpeggio pattern three. Turn your ear to the example on Track 112.

Track 112

Minor seven flat five arpeggio pattern 4

Arpeggio pattern 4 starts with your fourth finger on the root note and finishes with your third finger on the octave.

Follow the figure for notation, tab, and a neck diagram for the Dm7♭5 arpeggio pattern 4. Track 113 has the example.

Track 113

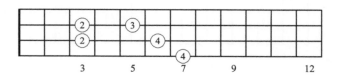

Moving around your minor seven flat five arpeggios

Patterns 1–4 that I describe in the preceding four sections are all moveable, meaning that you can move them up and down the neck and even across the strings to enable you to play any minor seven flat five arpeggio. For example, you can move any closed-pattern Am7♭5 arpeggio up two frets, and the same pattern becomes a Bm7♭5 arpeggio. You can also move the Am7♭5 arpeggio over one string to make a Dm7♭5 arpeggio.

The following figure shows a two measure Am7♭5 riff using the four moveable patterns: (a) pattern 1, (b) pattern 2, (c) pattern 3, and (d) pattern 4. Starting with pattern 1, memorize the riff in all four patterns. Play this sequence using all down-strokes with straight or not swinging eighth notes (quavers).

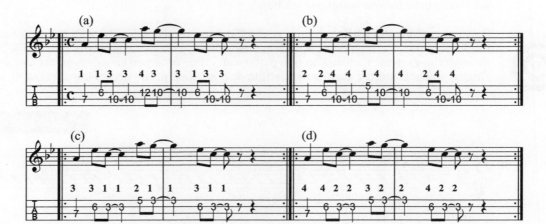

Now try to follow the chord progression in the next figure by playing the minor seven flat five riff to match the chords. Track 114 finds you sitting in with a virtual Afro-Cuban Jazz band. Follow me the first time through and then take it by yourself the second time. Try to stay in one region of the fingerboard by using a variety of patterns.

For example, start the exercise with the Am7♭5 sequence using pattern 3, with your third finger on the seventh fret of the d-string. For the Em7♭5 sequence, use pattern 4, which starts with your fourth finger on the ninth fret of the g-string. For the Bm7♭5 sequence, use pattern 1 starting with your first finger on the B note on the fourth fret of the g-string. For F♯m7♭5, you can simply move the Bm7♭5 pattern over one string higher (from the g-string to the d-string) and use pattern 1. For the Gm7♭5, use pattern 2 starting with your second finger on the G note located at the fifth fret of the d-string. For the Dm7♭5, use pattern 3, which starts with your third finger on the D note at the seventh fret of the g-string.

Tension and release

Usually, you don't play minor seven flat five chords/arpeggios by themselves (for example, as a chord that you'd strum in a folk song). You commonly use them, however, in jazz cadences or short chord progressions that move from chord to chord quickly, creating many little sections of tension to release.

With this method, you play through the complete exercise with your left hand, covering an area from fret three to fret ten. This region is known as *second position,* because your first finger is now playing frets usually played by your second finger. By staying in position, you become more efficient with your left hand.

If you have difficulty with the minor seven flat five exercise, play through the entire practice track using pattern 1, go back, and then memorize the riff using patterns 2, 3, and 4. Next go through the exercise focusing on one pattern at a time until you know where each arpeggio is. Finally, go back and try staying in position as described in the preceding paragraph.

Track 114

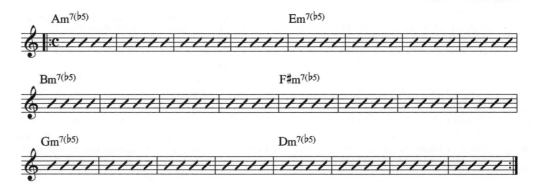

Staying focused on minor seven flat five arpeggios in open position

If playing jazz, tango, choro, or bossa nova on your mandolin interests you, spend some time becoming familiar with all the minor seven flat five arpeggios in open position. Many folks agree that the mandolin has its fullest, richest sound in open position.

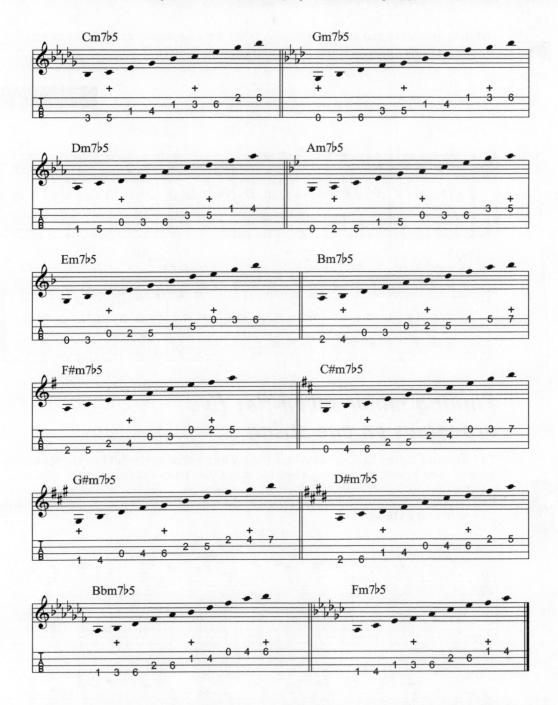

When you feel up to scratch on these open-position minor seven flat five arpeggios, try the following exercise. Bear in mind the four rules I identify in the earlier section 'Focusing on minor seventh arpeggios in open position'.

As so often, I place brackets over the transition notes that demonstrate good voice leading.

Listen to Track 115 and see the following figure for a demonstration of this exercise. The second time through I stop playing and you go it alone.

Track 115

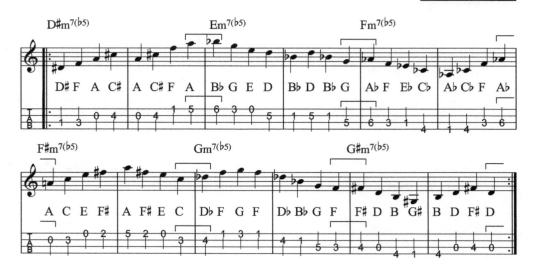

Finding minor seven flat five arpeggios on one string

The following figure demonstrates how to play four minor seven flat five chords/arpeggios without ever leaving the e-string. I include chord tone names above the tab.

Each arpeggio starts on the lowest possible chord tone on the e-string, not necessarily the root note of the chord.

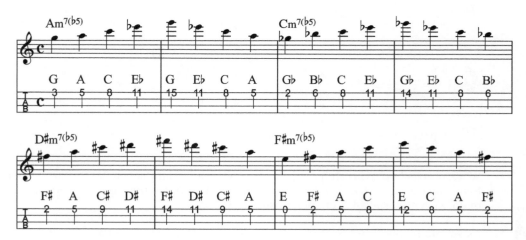

Connecting minor seven flat five arpeggio patterns: Two octaves

Here I demonstrate several common ways of playing two-octave minor seven flat five arpeggios.

The following two-octave Dm7♭5 arpeggio uses pattern 3 for the first octave, followed by pattern 1 for the higher octave. Note that the transition between the two octaves requires you to play two notes in a row with your first finger, which is a perfect opportunity to incorporate a slide (see *Mandolin For Dummies*) transition from one pattern to another.

See the following figure for notation, tab, and a neck diagram for the two-octave Dm7♭5 arpeggio 3-1.

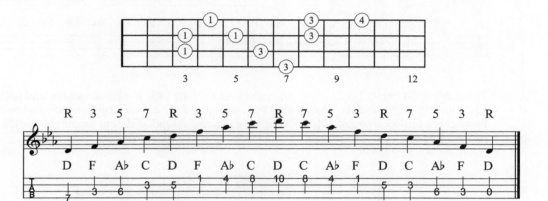

 Be sure to follow the proper fingerings. Finger numbers are the small numbers located inside the circles in the neck diagram. Proper fingerings are crucial for mastering these arpeggios.

The next two-octave Dm7♭5 arpeggio uses pattern 3 for the lower octave and pattern 2 for the second octave. Notice that this 3-2 two-octave pattern uses the same notes played at the same frets with a slightly different fingering from the two-octave pattern 3-1. A case of same sound, different fingering patterns – one that requires you to make a position shift, and one that requires you to use your fourth finger.

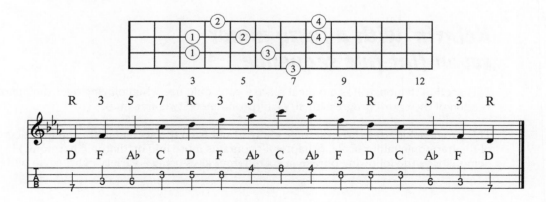

The pattern 2-1 two-octave Cm7♭5 arpeggio uses pattern 2 for the lower octave and pattern 1 for the higher octave. You have no position shift to worry about, which allows you to stay in position. See the following figure for notation, tab, and a neck diagram for this two-octave Cm7♭5 arpeggio pattern.

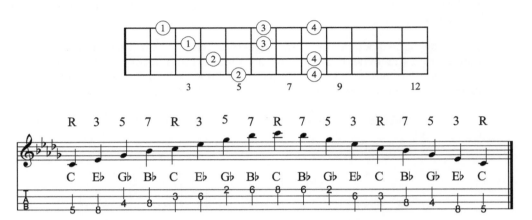

The pattern 1-1 two-octave Cm7♭5 arpeggio uses pattern 1 for the lower octave and pattern 1 again for the higher octave. Notice that the notes and frets are exactly the same as the previous two-octave Cm7♭5 arpeggio 2-1. Another case of same sound, different fingering. See the following figure for notation, tab, and a neck diagram for this arpeggio.

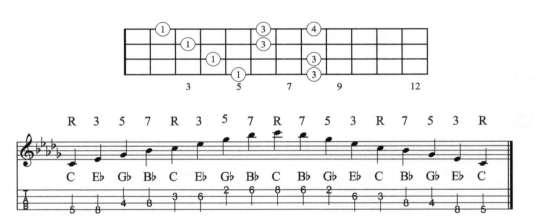

Relaxin' with a jazzy minor seven flat five sequence

This section demonstrates a typical phrase you could use when playing over the minor key version of the chord progression ii/V7/i/ (pronounced two–five–one).

This progression uses three diatonic chords built from the second, fifth, and first degrees of the harmonic minor scale. (Chapter 12 contains more info on diatonic harmony.) I demonstrate the following phrase in six different keys using a variety of arpeggio patterns.

Recognizing the patterns in this exercise is essential. You can see that I use brackets below the tab to illustrate the use of different patterns, and finger numbers above the tab to make the patterns and shifts easier to see and understand. Play this phrase using only down-strokes.

Track 116 features a jazzy bossa nova beat very similar to what was used on Track 95 to back you up. Like many of the other tracks, I lead you through the exercise first and then I hand it over to you.

Track 116

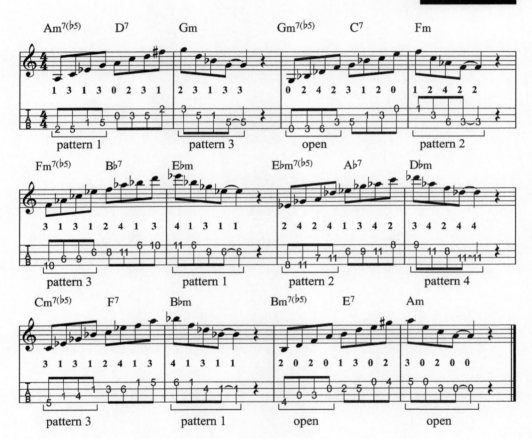

Chapter 11

Creating Drama with Diminished and Augmented Arpeggios

*N*o doubt you've come across certain pieces of music that sound a bit frightening. I don't mean in the sense of being frighteningly bad, like so much current pop! I'm thinking of great but unnerving, if not downright spooky, music like you would hear in Alfred Hitchcock's classic 'Psycho' or horror/thriller style movies scored by Bernard Hermann. Often musicians achieve this unsettling effect with diminished and augmented arpeggios, which create drama in classical music or are used as passing chords in jazz. Passing chord is a term that describes non-diatonic chords used to connect two diatonic chords. For example G/A♭dim7/Am7/B♭dim7/Bm7. The A♭dim7 and the B♭dim7 chords are not in the key of G major while the G, Am7 and Bm7 are. (See Chapter 12) When used as passing chords they don't seem very scary at all! Some musicians jokingly refer to these most dissonant of chords as 'demolished and argumentative chords'.

Sounding Spooky: Diminished Seventh Arpeggios — One Chord with Four Names

Whereas major chords often sound happy, and minor chords sad, diminished seventh (dim7) chords sound spooky. You can even say that they sound more minor than minor chords/arpeggios!

You can think of diminished seventh chords/arpeggios as two pairs of tritones (see Chapter 9) a minor third apart.

A diminished seventh chord/arpeggio is the result of a mathematical formula of four notes stacked in consecutive minor third intervals. For example, the Gdim7 chord contains the notes G, B♭, C♯, and E. Notice that the interval between each note is a minor third (or three frets), including the interval from E to the octave G. Chords/arpeggios built from intervals don't fit neatly into any scale, which is why they sound more mysterious or dissonant.

But wait, there's more! Each diminished seventh chord has four possible names as the title of this section suggests. Because the intervals or harmonic distance between each of the chord tones (notes in the chord) is exactly the same, you can stand this chord upside down on it's head and it is still the same chord! That means that G dim7, B♭ dim7, C♯ dim7, and E dim7 all contain exactly the same notes (G, B♭, C♯, E). One chord with four possible names. Knowing that there are a total of twelve notes in one octave of the chromatic scale (see Chapter 5) and that the diminished seventh chord contains four notes, with each one possibly being the root, you could come to the conclusion that there are really only three unique diminished seventh chords, each one with four possible names.

Look at the following chord tone table. You can see that Gdim7 includes G, B♭, C♯, and E, while B♭dim7 contains B♭, C♯, E, and G; C♯dim7 contains C♯, E, G, and B♭; and Edim7 contains E, G, B♭, and C♯.

As shown in the following chord table, only three different diminished seventh chords exist, each with four possible names.

Chord				
Cdim7	C	E♭	F♯	A
C♯dim7	C♯	E	G	B♭
Ddim7	D	F	A♭	B
E♭dim7	E♭	F♯	A	C
Edim7	E	G	B♭	C♯
Fdim7	F	A♭	B	D
F♯dim7	F♯	A	C	E♭
Gdim7	G	B♭	C♯	E
A♭dim7	A♭	B	D	F
Adim7	A	C	E♭	F♯
B♭dim7	B♭	C♯	E	G
Bdim7	B	D	F	A♭

Diminished seventh arpeggio diagonal pattern

By looking at the neck diagram in the following figure of the diminished seventh arpeggios, you can see two diagonal tritone patterns three frets (or a minor third) apart. Think of these arpeggios as two-finger arpeggios, primarily using fingers one and three, although in some cases you'd want to use fingers two and four.

Check out the following figure and Track 117 at www.dummies.com/go/mandolinexercises for the C–E♭–F♯–Adim7 arpeggios using the two-finger pattern and fingers one and three.

Track 117

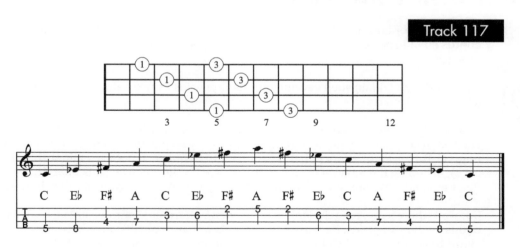

This exercise uses a cascading diminished seventh arpeggio sequence that follows the moveable diagonal pattern (shown earlier in this section). This sequence is a finger-buster for sure, which does require you to use all four fingers. Be sure to follow the finger numbers placed above the tablature (tab) and listen to Track 118 which has you playing your mandolin in a 1970's style disco band just for the fun of it.

Use alternate picking with your right hand for this tricky exercise. Notice that the sequences for Bdim7 and Ddim7 are identical. The same is true with Cdim7 and E♭dim7 and C♯dim7 and Edim7. (Remember that each diminished seventh arpeggio has four possible names.)

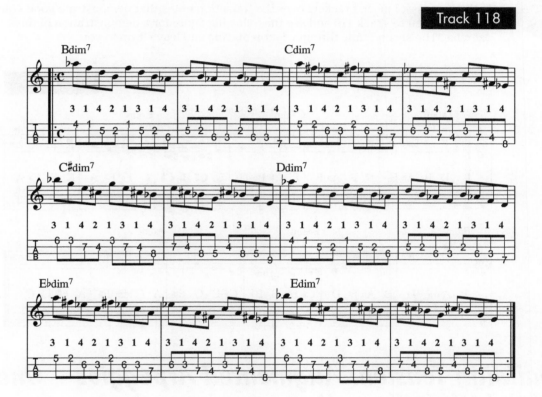

Track 118

Diminished seventh arpeggios in open position

As with all the other scales and arpeggios I demonstrate in this book, the best idea is to practice diminished seventh arpeggios in open position along with closed moveable patterns (which I explain in Chapter 3).

The great news is that you have only three patterns to learn because each pattern represents four chords/arpeggios: a diminished seventh chord can take the name of any of the four notes making up the chord/arpeggio.

When you have these open-position diminished seventh arpeggios under your fingers, try the following simple but challenging exercise, bearing in mind these few simple rules:

- ✔ **Stay in open position using open strings whenever possible.**
- ✔ **Follow the chord progression using only chord tones.**
- ✔ **Follow the chord progression using only quarter notes (crotchets).**
- ✔ **Use good voice leading (which I explain in Chapter 9) when transitioning from one chord to another.**

In this exercise, I place brackets over the transition notes that demonstrate good voice leading. Listen to Track 119 and see the following figure for a demonstration of this exercise. The second time through, I stop playing and leave it up to you.

Track 119

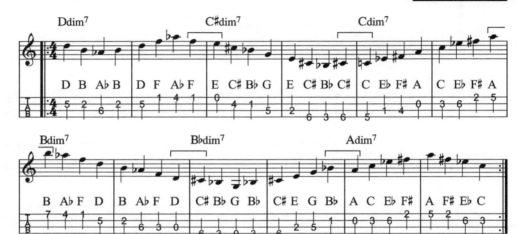

Building Tension: Augmented Arpeggios – One Chord With Three Names

Augmented chords/arpeggios have a very unsettled sound that seems to be asking for resolution. When used in context, augmented (aug) chords can also convey the feeling of movement. Dig out Beatles records and listen to the opening E augmented piano chord on the song 'Oh Darlin'.

An *augmented chord/arpeggio* is the result of a mathematical formula of three notes stacked in consecutive major third intervals. For example, the Gaug chord contains the notes G, B, and E♭. Notice that the distance between each note is a major third, or four frets. As with diminished seventh chords (see the earlier section 'Sounding Spooky: Diminished Seventh Arpeggios – One Chord with Four Names'), you can name the augmented chord with the name of any of the notes in the chord. Look to the following chord tone table to see that Caug, Eaug, and G♯aug all contain the same notes. So this group of three notes can be called Caug, Eaug, or G♯aug, depending on the function of the chord or the key of the composition. (Best to leave the worrying about chord names to the composers.)

Chord			
Caug	C	E	G#
C#aug	C#	F	A
Daug	D	F#	Bb
Ebaug	Eb	G	B
Eaug	E	G#	C
Faug	F	A	C#
F#aug	F#	Bb	D
Gaug	G	B	D#
G#aug	G#	C	E
Aaug	A	C#	F
Bbaug	Bb	D	F#
Baug	B	D#	G

Augmented arpeggio diagonal pattern

By looking at the neck diagram of the augmented arpeggios, you see two diagonal patterns running in the opposite direction to the diminished seventh arpeggios in the earlier 'Sounding Spooky: Diminished Seventh Arpeggios – One Chord with Four Names' section. The diagonal pattern of the augmented arpeggio uses the interval of a major third (or a span of four frets).

Think of these arpeggios as two-finger arpeggios primarily using fingers one and three, although in some cases you're better off using fingers two and four.

Listen to Track 120 and see the following figure for the notation, tab, and neck diagram for the augmented chord, which can be named A, C♯, F, or Aaug.

Track 120

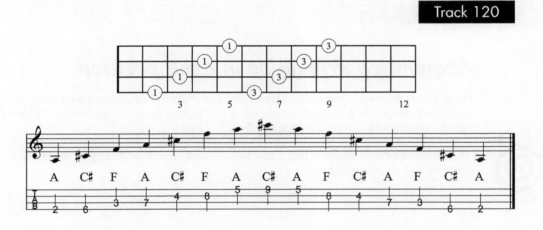

This exercise uses a simple augmented arpeggio sequence (or *lick*). By playing this lick in six different keys, you begin to see the augmented diagonal pattern on the mandolin fingerboard. Pay attention to the fingerings marked above the tab and listen to Track 121. Notice that Caug, Eaug, and G♯aug all contain the same notes. The same goes for Daug, F♯aug, and B♭aug.

Track 121 features our Afro-Cuban rhythm section again but this time they are laying down a rhythm known as the cha cha cha. Follow me the first time through and then I will stop playing, leaving it up to you.

Track 121

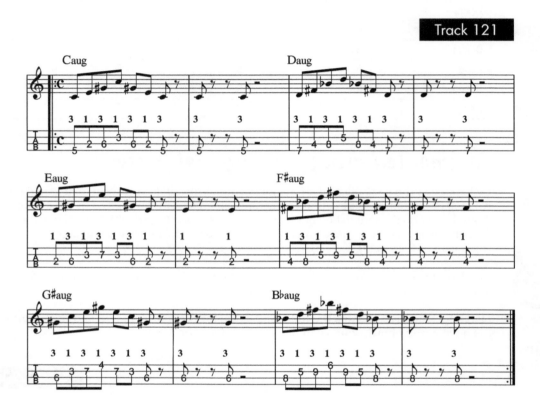

Augmented arpeggios in open position

Throughout this book you encounter more than once my rant about why open position is so important. Remember that you need to learn only four patterns (instead of 12) because each pattern represents three chords/arpeggios.

Like diminished chords, you can name augmented chords with any of the three notes that make up the chord/arpeggio.

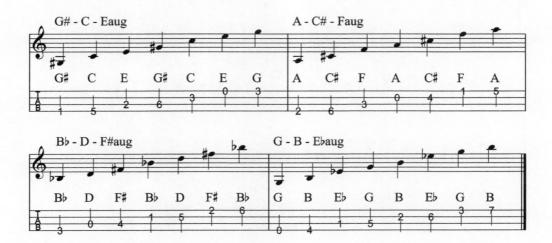

When you have these open-position augmented arpeggios flowing freely, try the following exercise. Don't forget to follow the simple rules that I list in the earlier section 'Diminished seventh arpeggios in open position'. I place brackets over the transition notes that demonstrate good voice leading.

Listen to Track 122 and see the figure for a demonstration of this exercise. The second time through I stop playing, leaving you to carry on alone.

Track 122

Part IV
Chords

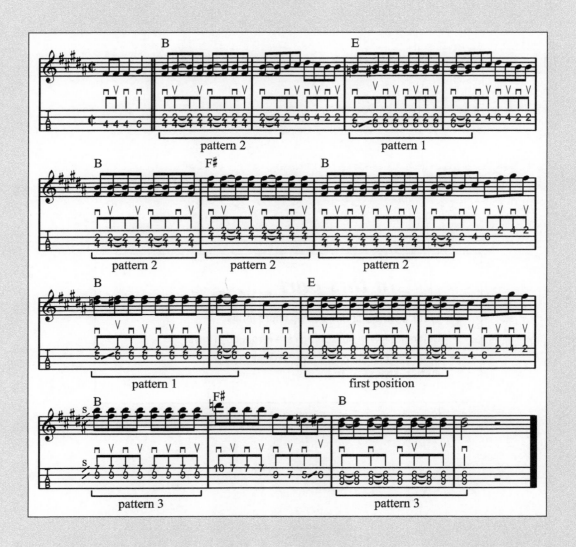

In this part . . .

✔ Crack a variety of three string chord forms.

✔ Get to grips with how chords are arranged in keys.

✔ Practise common chord progressions in various
   musical styles.

Chapter 12

Tying Everything Together: Diatonic Harmony

In This Chapter

▶ Understanding diatonic harmony

▶ Connecting arpeggios and major scales together

▶ Playing arpeggios in minor keys

*P*racticing different techniques in isolation is of course essential to building up your skills. But the real satisfaction and fun of playing mandolin comes when you start to join together these various aspects into a single piece.

This chapter collects the scales, chords, and arpeggios that I present throughout this book, grouping the various types of arpeggios by key.

Discovering the Delights of Diatonic Harmony

The musical term *diatonic* refers to notes or musical pitches that are of a scale. For example, if you're in the key of C major (which has no sharps or flats in the key signature), all the notes are natural and form the scale C, D, E, F, G, A, B, and C.

This group of notes is known as the C major scale and is used to create melodies, harmonies, counterpoint, bass lines, and chords. In general, all musical instruments – whether sung, plucked, bowed, blown, strummed, or smashed with your forehead – contain these same notes when you're in the key of C major.

Key is the term used to determine which scale is being used. So by knowing that a song is in the key of C major, you not only know that the C major scale is being used, but also the chords that are possible in that key.

Arpeggios are broken chords played one note at a time, and chords are built from scales. Arpeggios, chords, and scales are therefore all very closely related.

Play all the exercises in this chapter using alternate picking. If you aren't sure about this technique, check out *Mandolin For Dummies*. I show proper left-hand fingerings directly above the tablature, and include chord symbols to indicate the diatonic chords/arpeggios throughout the exercises. Try to memorize the diatonic chords and arpeggios for each key.

Playing Diatonic Triads in Major Keys

Major keys contain major chords, minor chords, and one diminished chord. The following table shows all seven of the diatonic *triads* (simple three-note chords) for each of the 12 major keys.

Key	I	ii	iii	IV	V	vi	vii
C	C	Dm	Em	F	G	Am	Bdim
D♭	D♭	E♭	Fm	G♭	A♭	B♭m	Cdim
D	D	Em	F#m	G	A	Bm	C#dim
E♭	E♭	Fm	Gm	A♭	B♭	Cm	Ddim
E	E	F#m	G#m	A	B	C#m	D#dim
F	F	Gm	Am	B♭	C	Dm	Edim
G♭	G♭	A♭m	B♭m	C♭	D♭	E♭m	Fdim
G	G	Am	Bm	C	D	Em	F#dim
A♭	A♭	B♭m	Cm	D♭	E♭	Fm	Gdim
A	A	Bm	C#m	D	E	F#m	G#dim
B♭	B♭	Cm	Dm	E♭	F	Gm	Adim
B	B	C#m	D#m	E	F#	G#m	A#dim

Pattern 1-4

The following sequence in the key of A major starts with your first finger on the A note, which is located at the second fret of the g-string. I demonstrate it on Track 123 at www.dummies.com/go/mandolinexercises.

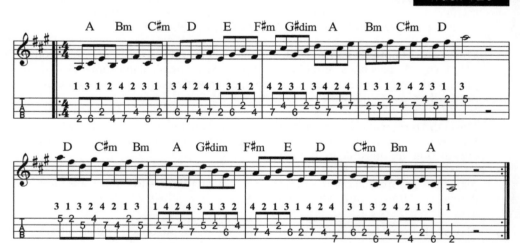

Pattern 2-1

The next sequence, which is in the key of C major, starts with your second finger on the C note at the fifth fret of the g-string. Listen to the demonstration on Track 124.

Track 124

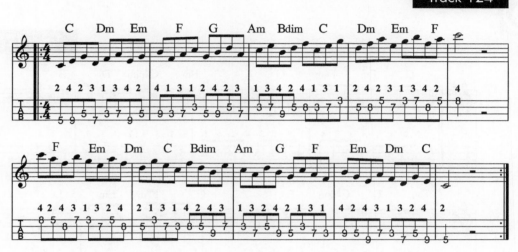

Pattern 3-2

This sequence is in the key of D major and starts with your third finger on the D note, which is at the seventh fret of the g-string. I demonstrate it on Track 125.

Track 125

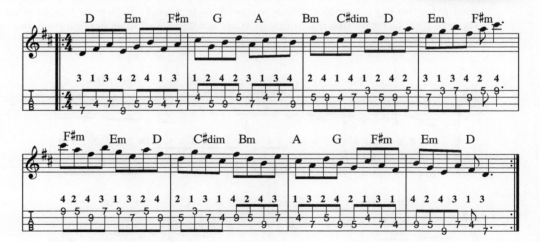

Pattern 4-3

To play this sequence, in the key of D major, start with your fourth finger on the D note at the seventh fret of the g-string. Check out Track 126 for a demonstration.

Notice that the preceding figure was in D major using pattern 3-2, while this exercise is in D major using pattern 4-3.

Track 126

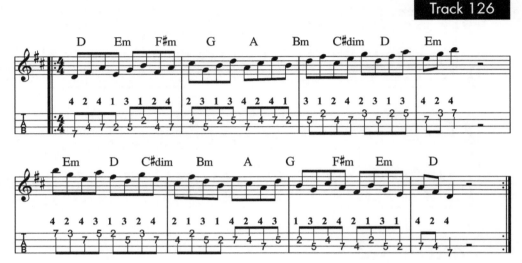

Opening up: Diatonic major triads in open position

The following figure shows the diatonic triads in open position using open strings where possible for the key of G major. When you see how this works in G, your task (if you choose to accept it) is to figure this major key diatonic sequence out in as many keys using open position as you can.

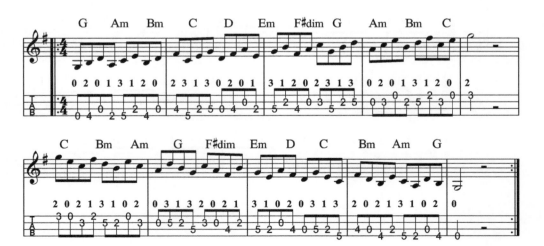

Setting about Diatonic Sevenths in Major Keys

Seventh chords are simply four-note chords/arpeggios (as you can see in Chapter 10). When applied to seventh chords, the term diatonic means that the chords are constructed from major or minor scales. Major keys contain a variety of four-note chord types, including Maj7, m7, seventh, and m7♭5. The following table shows you all the diatonic seventh chords in all 12 major keys.

Key	I	ii	iii	IV	V	vi	vii
C	Cmaj7	Dm7	Em7	Fmaj7	G7	Am7	Bm7♭5
D♭	D♭maj7	E♭m7	Fm7	G♭maj7	A♭7	B♭m7	Cm7♭5
D	Dmaj7	Em7	F#m7	Gmaj7	A7	Bm7	C#m7♭5
E♭	E♭maj7	Fm7	Gm7	A♭maj7	B♭7	Cm7	Dm7♭5
E	Emaj7	F#m7	G#m7	Amaj7	B7	C#m7	D#m7♭5
F	Fmaj7	Gm7	Am7	B♭maj7	C7	Dm7	Em7♭5
G♭	G♭maj7	A♭m7	B♭m7	C♭maj7	D♭7	E♭m7	Fm7♭5
G	Gmaj7	Am7	Bm7	Cmaj7	D7	Em7	F#m7♭5
A♭	A♭maj7	B♭m7	Cm7	D♭maj7	E♭7	Fm7	Gm7♭5
A	Amaj7	Bm7	C#m7	Dmaj7	E7	F#m7	G#m7♭5
B♭	B♭maj7	Cm7	Dm7	E♭maj7	F7	Gm7	Am7♭5
B	Bmaj7	C#m7	D#m7	Emaj7	F#7	G#m7	A#m7♭5

Pattern 1-4

The following sequence, which is in the key of A major, starts with your first finger on the A note at the second fret of the g-string. I demonstrate it on Track 127.

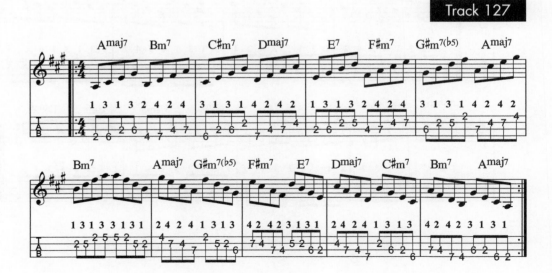

Pattern 2-1

The next sequence is in the key of C major. Start with your second finger on the C note, at the fifth fret of the g-string, and listen to the demonstration on Track 128.

Track 128

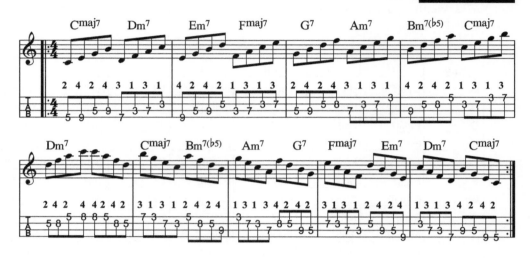

Pattern 3-2

Start playing the following sequence (in the key of D major) with your third finger on the D note at the seventh fret of the g-string. You can hear the exercise played on Track 129.

Track 129

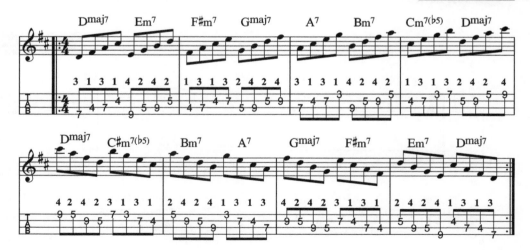

Pattern 4-3

This sequence is in the key of D major and starts with your fourth finger on the D note located at the seventh fret of the g-string. Listen to Track 130 for a demonstration.

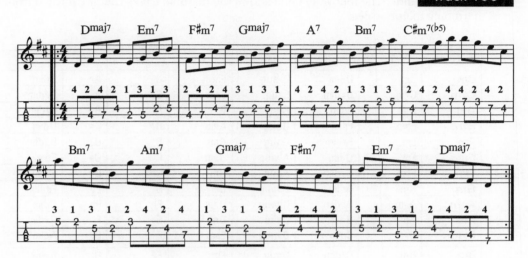

Practicing diatonic seventh arpeggios in open position

The following figure shows the diatonic seventh arpeggios in open position using open strings where possible for the key of A major. When you have a handle on these diatonic seventh arpeggios in A, try figuring them out in as many keys as you can.

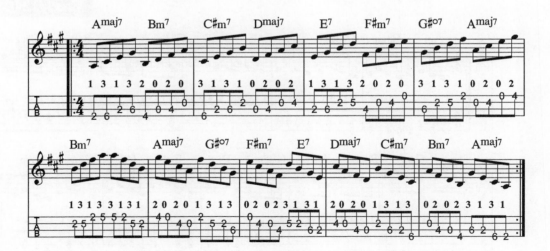

Trying out Diatonic Triads in Harmonic Minor Keys

You can build diatonic triads from major scales or minor scales. Harmonic minor scales have a very exotic sound, and the chords/arpeggios that are derived from these scales are a bit on the dark side. The following table shows the diatonic triads that are formed from the harmonic minor scales.

Key	i	ii	III	iv	V	VI	vii
Cm	Cm	Ddim	E♭aug	Fm	G	A♭	Bdim
C#m	C#m	D#dim	Eaug	F#m	G#	A	B#dim
Dm	Dm	Edim	Faug	Gm	A	B♭	C#dim
E♭m	E♭m	Fdim	Gaug	A♭m	B♭	C♭	Ddim
Em	Em	F#dim	Gaug	Am	B	C	D#dim
Fm	Fm	Gdim	A♭aug	B♭m	C	D♭	Edim
F#m	F#m	G#dim	Aaug	Bm	C#	D#	E#dim
Gm	Gm	Adim	B♭aug	Cm	D	E♭	F#dim
A♭m	A♭m	B♭dim	C♭aug	D♭m	E♭	F♭	Gdim
Am	Am	Bdim	Caug	Dm	E	F	G#dim
B♭m	B♭m	Cdim	D♭aug	E♭m	F	G♭	Adim
Bm	Bm	C#dim	Daug	Em	F#	G	Adim

Pattern 1-4

The following figure, which is in the key of A harmonic minor, starts with your first finger on the A note at the second fret of the g-string. I demonstrate it on Track 131.

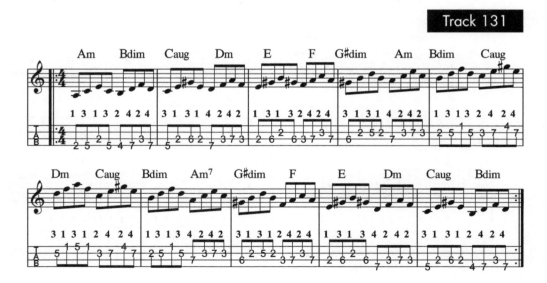

Track 131

Pattern 2-1

The following sequence is in the key of C harmonic minor. You start with your second finger on the C note at the fifth fret of the g-string. Check out Track 132.

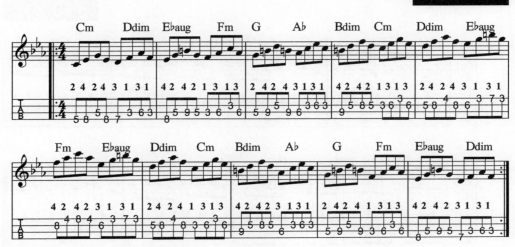

Pattern 3-2

Start playing the following exercise in the key of D harmonic minor with your third finger on the D note at the seventh fret of the g-string. You can hear it on Track 133.

Pattern 4-3

The following sequence is also in the key of D harmonic minor. Start with your fourth finger on the D note located at the seventh fret of the g-string, and listen to the demonstration on Track 134.

Track 134

Uncovering diatonic minor triads in open position

The following figure shows the diatonic triads in open position using open strings where possible, for the key of G harmonic minor. When you grasp how this works in G harmonic minor, try figuring it out in as many harmonic minor keys as you can.

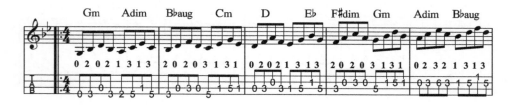

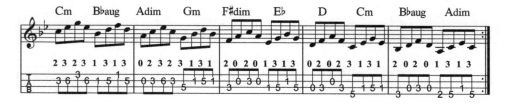

Chapter 13

Seeing that Less Is More with Three-String Closed Chords

*P*eople often state that 'less is more' – usually employers trying to get you to accept a pay cut! But the saying's certainly true as regards three-string chords. Why mess around with trying to twist your fingers around to make four string chords when you can get the job done with simple, easy to make, great sounding three-string chords?

Being able to use the three-string chording method for mandolin allows you to expand greatly your chord possibilities, so that the next time you're playing in a jam session and the guitarist puts the capo on fret three and announces 'This one's in B♭', you can hold your head high and know that mandolin players can play in B♭, E♭, or any other key by using this three-string method (which I explain in detail in Chapter 7 of *Mandolin For Dummies*).

This chapter contains exercises in the various forms of major, minor, seventh, diminished, and augmented chords that you play using only three adjacent strings. I demonstrate the chord forms on lower (bass) strings and higher (treble) strings, because you want to be able to play chords in all ranges of your instrument, and due to the way the mandolin is tuned, you can simply move chord forms from the lower three adjacent strings to the higher three adjacent strings. They become different chords but the form or shape remains the same. For example: The D chord (root note on top) is played on the three lower strings (g,d,a) using frets 2,4, and 5. By locking your fingers and just moving them over one string higher (d,a,e) you are making an A chord. Try that with a guitar, banjo or uke!

The neck diagrams in this chapter don't use standard fingering notation. This chapter is all about learning chord forms and their relationship to each other, and so the numbers inside the white circular fret indicators represent the chord form, not the fingerings. (I show the latter at the bottom of the chord diagrams.) So a neck diagram showing a chord form with the number 1 is for form one, 3 is for form three, and 5 is for form five.

Remember to download the audio tracks for this book at www.dummies.com/go/ mandolinexercises. You will benefit greatly from hearing these exercises before attempting to play them. In addition, I design many of the tracks so that you can play along with a rhythm section.

Brushing up on Chord Theory 101

This chapter pulls together many of the skills and much of the wisdom I present throughout this book. In order to master the three-string chord *inversions* (or chord forms) on the mandolin, you need a good understanding of the three following concepts:

- ✔ **Three moveable, three-string major chord forms:** Covered in detail in Chapter 7 of *Mandolin For Dummies*.
- ✔ **An understanding of the notes on the mandolin from the nut to the 12th fret of each string:** Check out the neck diagram in Chapter 1.
- ✔ **An understanding of *chord tones:*** Notes that make up major, minor, sevenths, diminished, and augmented chords. I include chord tone tables in Chapters 7–11.

To get the most out of this chapter, you need to understand basic chord theory and grasp the concept that A, C♯, and E make what's known as an A major chord. In Chapters 7–11, I look at these note groups as arpeggios, which are simply chords played one note at a time. In this chapter you encounter *chord shapes:* forms in which all the notes in the chord can be simultaneously played by strumming or by using cross-picking patterns or any number of rhythm patterns.

The exercises presented in this chapter use rhythm notation. This style of notation is commonly used by musicians in the rhythm section of a band or orchestra, and is a bit different than standard notation or tablature. At the top of the stem where the note head (the part that indicates what note you are to play) would normally be, is either a slash or an x. These rhythm slashes or x's can be written as eighth notes, quarter notes, dotted notes or any other rhythmic value you would use when writing standard notation or tab. The only difference is that there are no actual pitch values. The slash indicates a strum and an x indicates a muted strum, where you still strum the strings with your pick but you mute the strings by releasing the pressure on the strings with your left hand fingers just enough so the notes don't ring. This scratching technique is covered in *Mandolin For Dummies* and is an important element to playing good rhythm mandolin.

Discovering Three Major and Minor Inversions

Inversions are simply different ways of stacking from low to high; that is, organizing the notes of a chord. For example: The G chord contains the notes G, B, and D. It does not matter which one of these three notes is the bass note (lowest note) or which one is the highest note or even which one is the middle note. All that matters is that the notes G, B, and D are being played together.

Inverting major chords

I now look into inversions of major chords. If you need a refresher on three string major chords, turn to Chapter 7 of *Mandolin For Dummies*.

Take the example of the A major chord, which is made up of the notes A, C♯, and E. On a piano, you have countless variations of these three notes, because of the range and the way the keyboard allows you to play notes close together or far apart. But the way that the mandolin is tuned means that certain very close intervals and even some very great intervals aren't possible.

Consider the A major chord, starting with the A note at the second fret of the g-string. The next chord tone is C♯, which is on the sixth fret of the g-string. Having two chord tones on the same string is fine for arpeggios (see Chapters 7–11), but this chapter deals with chords where the notes are sounded simultaneously, and so each chord tone needs to be on a separate and adjacent string. Try adding the E note located at the second fret of the d-string, followed by the C♯ located at the fourth fret of the a-string. The notes in order from low to high are A, E, and C♯.

Now, three separate notes form the A major chord (or indeed any major or minor triad; see Chapter 7). Therefore, three possible top (or highest) pitches are available for each three-note chord (triad), and four possible top notes are available for seventh chords (because seventh chords contain four notes). The chords I provide in this chapter are organized into high-string versions (d-, a-, and e-strings) and low-string versions (g-, d-, and a-strings). Each group contains chord forms named for the top note.

Lower strings

The following figure shows the three inversions for the A major chord, using only the g-, d-, and a-strings, which are the three lowest strings of the mandolin.

I place the numbers 1, 3, and 5 next to the chord symbols to indicate one (root) on top, third on top, or fifth on top. Practice all three of these major chord forms, making sure that each note rings clear.

You can play only three strings while avoiding the e-string in two ways:

✓ **Mute the e-string by slightly flattening out whichever finger is playing the a-string, so that it touches the open e-string preventing it from ringing when you strum the strings.** Use not enough pressure to fret a note on the e-string, but enough to mute or deaden the e-string. Strum all four strings. You should hear three strings ring and just the dead click sound of the pick brushing the e string but no actual note from the e-string.

✓ **Learn to strum only three strings.** Avoid the e-string altogether.

The following figure shows neck diagrams for the chords A, D, G, and C major. Remember that the numbers are an indication of which form to use and *not* which finger to use. Practice all three versions of each chord starting at the nut and working your way up the neck, making sure that each note rings clear.

A
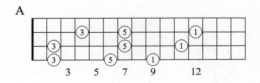

D
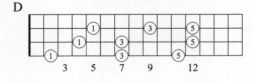

G
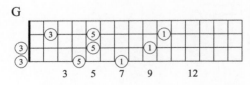

C
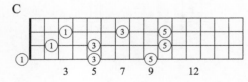

This exercise uses three major chord forms located on the low strings, played with a rhythm pattern based on a Cuban rhythm called *clave* (pronounced clah-vay) that has made its way into many forms of popular music. You need to have a good understanding of alternate picking/strumming and to be able to mute with your left hand while maintaining the rhythm pattern with your right hand. This muting technique results in a percussive sound with no pitch or note. This type of two-measure clave rhythm features two beats in the first measure and three beats in the second, and is simply called 2-3 clave.

Listen to Track 135 to see how this exercise works, and then jump in and have some fun with this Latin beat. Be sure to follow the chord diagrams. Watch for repeat signs at the end of each system or line. System is a term used in music notation or tab for one line of music.

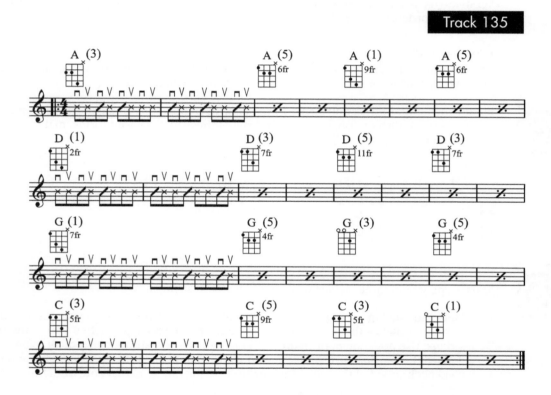

Higher strings

You can apply the same three major chord forms that you use on the lower strings (see the preceding section) to the higher strings.

The following figure shows the three inversions for the A major chord, using only the d-, a-, and e-strings (the three highest strings of the mandolin). Practice each chord form, making sure that each note is clear.

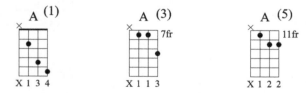

Not everyone uses the same fingerings for the same chord forms. I suggest using fingers 1, 2, and 4 for major chord form 1, but some people use fingers 1, 2, and 3.

The neck diagrams in the following figure demonstrate the high-string versions of the four major chords A, D, G, and C. Notice how both A and G start with form 1 followed by forms 3 and 5 as you move up the neck, whereas D starts on form 3, and C starts on form 5. Practice all three versions of each chord: start at the nut and work your way up the neck, always making sure that each note rings clear.

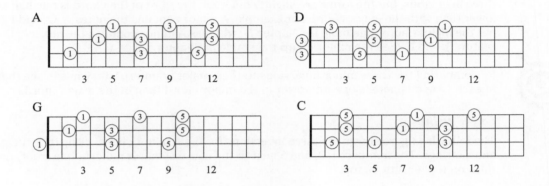

This exercise uses three major chord forms located on the high strings, based on the Cuban clave rhythm. This type of two-measure clave rhythm features three beats in the first measure and two beats in the second, and is simply called 3-2 clave. Be sure to follow marked pick direction and mute all strums with an 'x' at the top of the stem.

Track 136 shows how this exercise works. I supply a demonstration the first time and then stop playing, allowing you to play this Latin groove on your own.

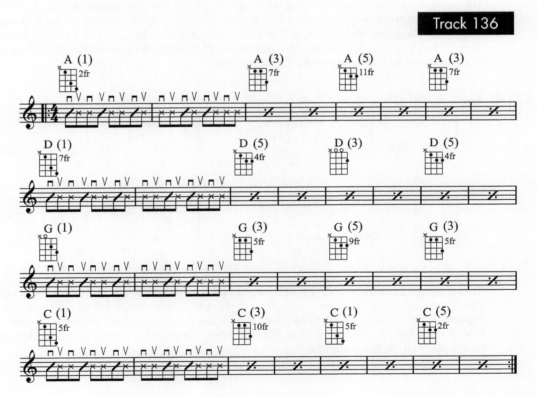

The exercises in this section are for the chords A, D, G, and C, but 12 possible major, minor, seventh, chords exist, with multiple forms of each chord. Challenge yourself to memorize all 12 of each chord type using this linear three-string approach.

Becoming sadder with three minor inversions

Like major chords (see the earlier section 'Inverting major chords'), minor chords also use three inversions, but the forms are slightly different: the third of the chord is one half step lower than with the major chord. For example, A major contains the notes A, C♯, and E (check out the major chord tone table in Chapter 7), whereas A minor contains the notes A, C (natural), and E. (See the minor chord tone table in Chapter 8.)

By comparing the three minor inversions to their major counterparts, you can see that in each case one note is one fret lower in the minor chord than in the major chord.

Lower strings

The following figure shows the three inversions for the A minor chord, using only the g-, d-, and a-strings. The numbers 1, 3, and 5 next to the chord symbols indicate one (root) on top, third on top, or fifth on top.

The neck diagrams in the following figure demonstrate the four minor chords Am, Dm, Gm, and Cm. Each neck diagram shows the one (root), three, and five forms of each chord while staying on the g-, d-, and a-strings. The forms are indicated by 1, 3, and 5 placed in the white circular fret indicators. Practice all three forms of one minor chord until you can play them from memory, before going on to the next chord.

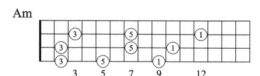 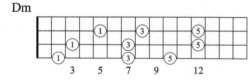

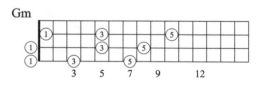 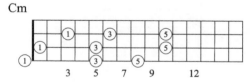

This exercise uses three-string minor chords on the lower strings, with a rhythm used in vintage swing music. This four-to-the-bar rhythm style with left-hand muting was a standard figure for the rhythm guitarist that played with the great gypsy guitar player Django Reinhardt. Check out Chapter 13 of *Mandolin For Dummies* for a variety of jazz rhythms that work well on the mandolin.

Listen first and then play along with Track 137 in the style of 1930s gypsy swing. Notice the dots placed directly above the rhythm slashes. These are called staccato marks, meaning to leave a bit of space or silence between each note or strum. This is accomplished by releasing the left hand pressure ever so slightly, stopping the chord from ringing. You can clearly hear this on the demonstration track.

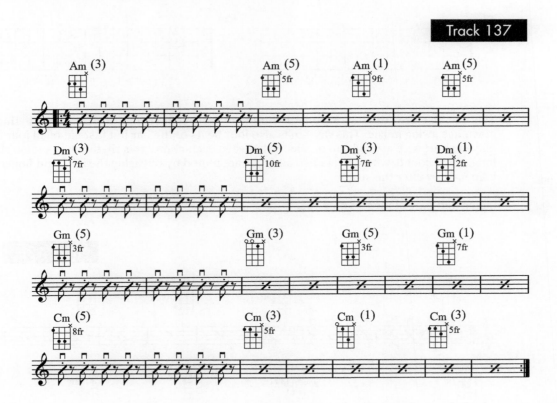

Higher strings

The following figure shows the three inversions for the A minor chord, using only the three highest strings of the mandolin: d, a, and e.

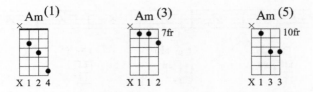

The neck diagrams in the following figure demonstrate the four minor chords Am, Dm, Gm, and Cm. Each neck diagram shows the one (root), three, and five forms of each chord while staying on the d-, a-, and e-strings. The forms are indicated by 1, 3, and 5 in the white circular fret indicators. Practice all three forms of one minor chord until you can play them from memory, and then go on to the next chord.

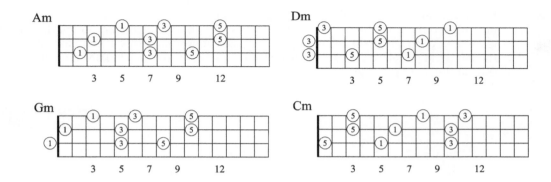

This exercise uses three-string minor chords on the higher strings, with another rhythm used in vintage swing music. This rhythm is also four beats to the bar but instead of all four being played short with a small gap or silence between each chord, this rhythm has a long, short, long, short sound, where beats two and four are muted by releasing the left-hand fingers immediately after the strum.

Listen and play along to Track 138.

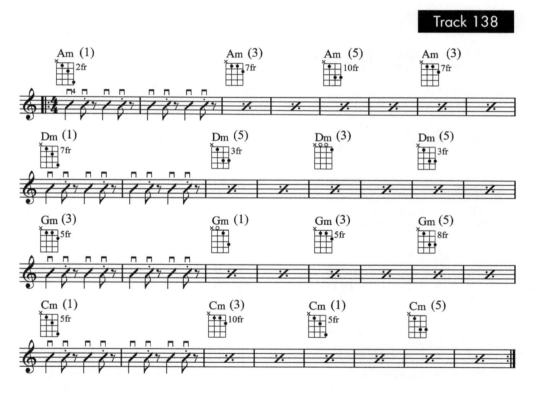

Playing in Seventh Heaven with Seventh Chord Inversions

Seventh chords are simple triads (see Chapters 7 & 8) with an additional note added to them giving these chords more color and depth. As you saw in the previous section, there are multiple ways to play the same chord and this applies to seventh chords also.

Feeling groovy with major sevenths

In Chapter 10, you discover that major seventh (maj7) chords/arpeggios contain four notes, which is all fine and dandy until you try to strum the chord only using three strings. By using only three strings, you omit one of the tones in the chord; this is no problem, and you don't need to worry about being arrested by the chord tone police. As a mandolin player, you need to understand that the mandolin is an instrument in a specific range (same as the violin), and some of its characteristic sounds that you love so much come from those limitations. One of those limitations is chording, so instead of tying your fingers in knots trying to cover all of the notes in a particular chord, many of the worlds best mandolin players use this three-string chording approach.

Another reason not to worry too much about playing only three notes of a chord is that when playing in a group or ensemble, someone else, such as the guitar, piano, or bass, is almost certainly playing that fourth note. This type of sound is more pleasing and complex, because each instrument is part of a collective sound instead of each one trying to cover everything. Chapter 7 of *Mandolin For Dummies* is devoted to these three-string mandolin chords.

Lower strings

The following figure shows the three inversions or chord forms for the Amaj7 chord, using only the g-, d-, and a-strings. Notice that I place the numbers 3, 5, and 7 next to the chord symbols to indicate third on top, fifth on top, or seventh on top.

A^maj7 (3)

1 2 4 x

A^maj7 (5)

6fr

1 1 2 x

A^maj7 (7)

9fr

1 3 3 X

The neck diagrams in the following figure demonstrate three major seventh chords. Each neck diagram shows the three, five, and seven forms of each chord while staying on the g-, d-, and a-strings. I indicate the forms with 3, 5, or 7 in the white circular fret indicators. Practice all three forms of each chord until you can play them from memory, and only then go on to the next chord.

Searching for a home

Upon close examination, you find that the Amaj7 chord forms are the same as those called a C♯ minor earlier in the 'Discovering Three Major and Minor Inversions' section. Amaj7 contains the notes A, C♯, E, and G♯, and C♯ minor contains the notes C♯, E, and G♯. In most forms of music, the bass player or lowest instrument in the group (guitar, piano, bass) is responsible for playing the root note of the chord, and so if the bass player or even the guitar player plays an A note and you're playing C♯, E, and G♯, your combined efforts make the complete Amaj7 chord. All the three-string maj7 inversions I describe in this chapter are rootless, meaning that the root note is the one deleted.

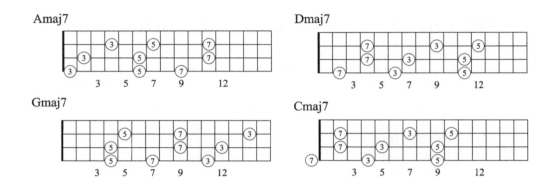

The following exercise is a one-measure rhythm pattern that's useful in bossa novas and other Brazilian-influenced grooves. Be sure to follow pick-direction marks (above the notation) and left-hand muting marks (x's). The chord diagrams indicate the chord form to play.

I demonstrate this exercise on Track 139.

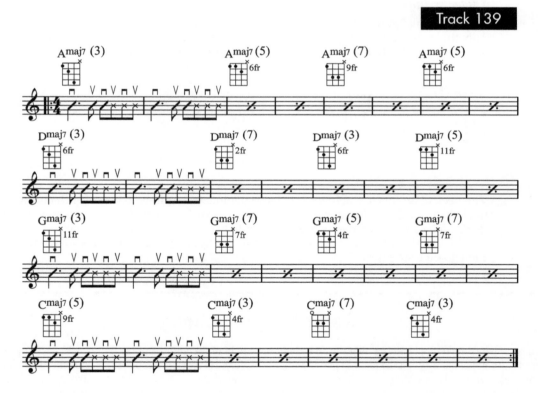

Higher strings

The following figure shows the three inversions for the Amaj7 chord, using only the d-, a-, and e-strings. The numbers 3, 5, and 7 next to the chord symbols indicate which note of the chord is on top.

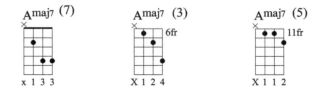

The neck diagrams in the following figure demonstrate three major seventh chords. Each neck diagram shows the three, five, and seven forms of each chord on the d-, a-, and e-strings. The forms are in the white circular fret indicators (3, 5, or 7). Practice all three forms of each chord until you can play them from memory, before moving on to the next chord.

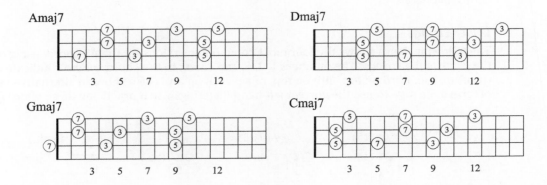

This exercise features three-string major seventh chords played with a pseudo-Brazilian strumming pattern in the mandolin tune 'Mr Natural', which I demonstrate in Chapter 13 of *Mandolin For Dummies*.

Play along with Track 140 using this funky, hippy, bossa-style groove.

Pay attention to the pick direction in this one! It is not simply alternate strumming but a strumming style where the direction of the pick (up or down) is dependant on the accent of the beat. Notice that all of the strums where you actually hear the chord are played with a down-stroke and all of the muted strokes are played with an up-stroke. Try playing only the down-strokes first adding the up-strokes once you have the basic rhythm mastered.

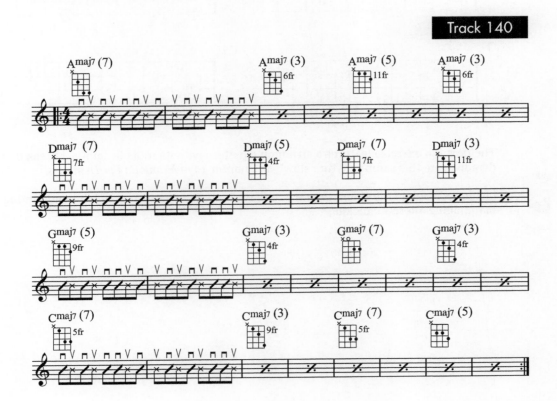

Knowing four dominant seventh inversions

Dominant seventh chords, commonly called seventh chords, contain four notes. (See the dominant chord tone table in Chapter 9.) This section demonstrates dominant seventh chord inversions.

Lower strings

The following figure shows the four most common inversions for the A7 chord, using only the g-, d-, and a-strings. The numbers 1, 3, 5, and 7 next to the chord symbols indicate one (root) on top, third on top, fifth on top, or seventh on top. I also show an alternative version of form 3. Be sure to use the correct left-hand fingerings when practicing these chord forms.

The neck diagrams in the following figure demonstrate four seventh chords. Each neck diagram shows the one (root), three, five, and seven forms of each chord while staying on the g-, d-, and a-strings. The forms are indicated by 1, 3, 5, and 7 placed in the white circular fret indicators. Practice all four forms of each chord until you can play them from memory, and only then proceed to the next chord.

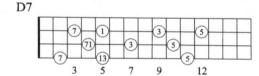

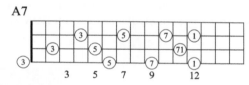 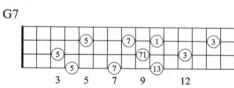

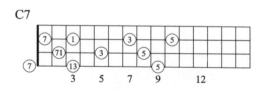

The next fun exercise features a strumming pattern with its roots in samba. I break down and demonstrate this samba rhythm slowly in Chapter 14 of *Mandolin For Dummies*.

Listen to Track 141 first and then try to play along. This pattern uses left-hand muting while maintaining alternate picking.

Track 141

Higher strings

The following figure shows the four most common inversions or chord forms for the A7 chord, using only the d-, a-, and e-strings. Notice that the numbers 1, 3, 5, and 7 next to the chord symbols indicate one (root) on top, third on top, fifth on top, or seventh on top. I also show an alternative version of form 3.

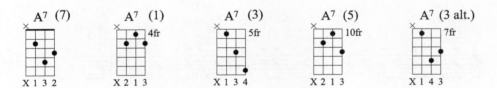

The neck diagrams in the following figure demonstrate the four most common dominant seventh chords. Each neck diagram shows the one (root), three, five, and seven forms of each chord while staying on the d-, a-, and e-strings. The forms are shown by 1, 3, 5, and 7 in the white circular fret indicators. Practice all four forms of each chord until you can play them from memory, and then go on to the next chord.

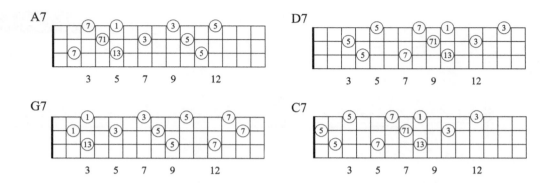

Who says you can't get funky on a mandolin? Watch the pick direction and the 'x's that indicate to mute the strings with your left hand while strumming with your right hand. I cover this scratching technique in Chapter 14 of *Mandolin For Dummies*.

Listen to Track 142 for a funky mandolin groove that works for a variety of popular music.

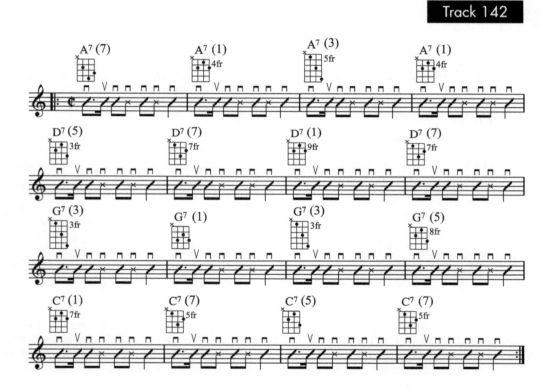

Moving on up the neck with four minor seventh inversions

Minor seventh (m7) chords contain four notes. (See the chord tone table in Chapter 10.) This section demonstrates minor seventh three-string chord inversions. Remember that in each chord form, one chord tone is missing because you're playing only three notes. Dropping out the root or the fifth of the chord is more common than eliminating the third or the seventh, which are the color tones. These tones are called color tones because they do just that in that they can change the color or feeling of the chord and the music it is used in. The third of the chord determines it's major or minor properties (happy or sad) while the seventh in the chord can convey motion, (dominant seventh chords) or stability (major seventh chords).

Lower strings

The following figure shows the four primary inversions and one alternative inversion for the Am7 chord, using only the g-, d-, and a-strings. The numbers 1, 3, 5, and 7 next to the chord symbols indicate one (root) on top, third on top, fifth on top, or seventh on top.

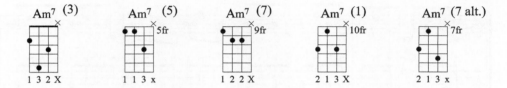

The neck diagrams in the following figure demonstrate four minor seventh chords. Each neck diagram shows the one (root), three, five, and seven forms of each chord while staying on the g-, d-, and a-strings. The forms are shown by the numbers 1, 3, 5, or 7 placed in the white circular fret indicators.

Practice making a smooth transition from one form to another.

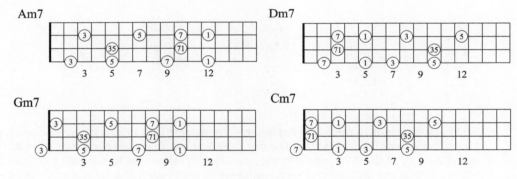

Here's an exercise that uses minor seventh chords and a non-strumming style of accompaniment. This arpeggiated chord style works great in ballads or slow songs. If you have trouble maintaining proper pick direction on this one, review some of the right-hand warm-up exercises in Chapter 2.

Play along with this exercise on Track 143.

Track 143

Higher strings

The following figure shows inversions for the Am7 chord, using only the d-, a-, and e-strings. I place the numbers 1, 3, 5, and 7 next to the chord symbols to indicate one (root) on top, third on top, fifth on top, or seventh on top.

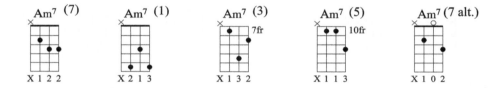

The neck diagrams in the following figure demonstrate four primary minor seventh chord forms. Each neck diagram shows the one (root), three, five and seven forms of each chord while staying on the d-, a-, and e-strings. As always, I show the forms with 1, 3, 5, or 7 in the white circular fret indicators. Practice all four forms of each chord until you can play them from memory, and then go on to the next chord.

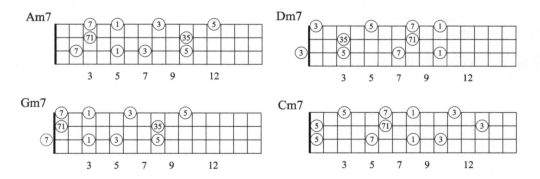

The following exercise uses dominant seventh chords in addition to minor seventh chords. You may want to read up on the dominant seventh chord forms I describe earlier in this chapter in 'Knowing four dominant seventh inversions'.

The following minor seventh chord exercise uses a simple Brazilian choro rhythm. Pay close attention to the pick direction and the fact that beat one is a muted or percussive sound.

This pattern doesn't adhere to standard alternate picking/strumming rules. In this Brazilian rhythm style the pick direction is more based on accents than which beat the strum lands on. All accented beats are played with down-strokes regardless of what beat they land on. Remember in alternate picking and strumming, the string beats (numbered beats) are played with down strokes and the weak beats (the ands) are played with upstrokes.

Listen to Track 144 before you try to play this pattern, because hearing the sound can be more helpful than using the sheet music alone. Watch for repeat signs at the end of each system or line.

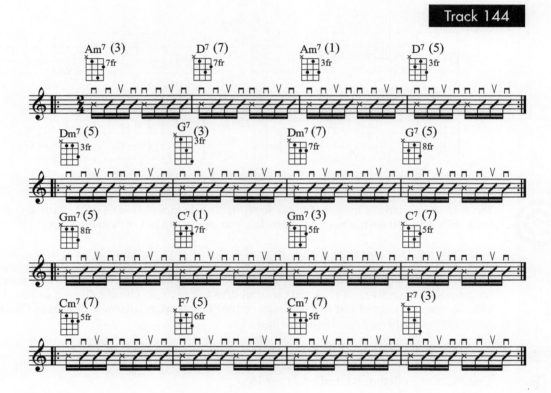

Understanding minor seventh flat five chord inversions

Minor seventh flat five (m7♭5) chords are halfway between a minor seventh chord and a diminished chord. In fact many people call this type of chord half-diminished. If you look at the root third and fifth of one of these chords you will find a diminished triad. By adding the minor seventh note this chord is no longer considered diminished. These chords very often function as a ii chord in a harmonic minor key. You can learn about diminished chords in Chapter 11.

Lower strings

The following figure shows the four inversions plus one alternative for the Am7♭5 chord, using only the g-, d-, and a-strings. The numbers 1, 3, 5, and 7 next to the chord symbols indicate which chord tone is the highest note in the chord.

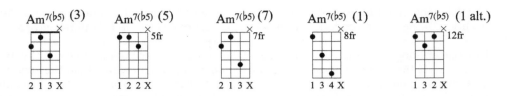

The neck diagrams in the following figure demonstrate four primary m7♭5 chords. Each neck diagram shows the one (root), three, five and seven forms of each chord while staying on the g-, d-, and a-strings. The forms are shown by 1, 3, 5, or 7 in the white circular fret indicators. Practice all four forms of each chord until you can play them from memory, and then move on to the next chord.

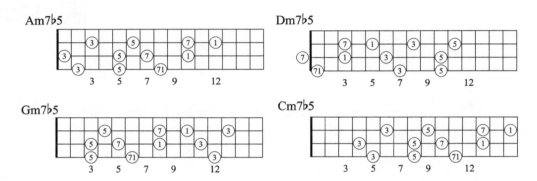

The following exercise uses dominant seventh chords in addition to m7♭5 chords. (I discuss these forms in the earlier section 'Knowing four dominant seventh inversions'.)

This exercise finds you in a swingin' jazz quartet. The rhythm figure or pattern is often called the Charleston, and you play it using all down-strokes. Try applying this cool rhythm to the ii7♭5/V7 (commonly called a minor two-five) chord progression in four keys. This chord progression is simply the (ii7 chord) second diatonic seventh chord followed by the (V7) the fifth diatonic seventh chord of a harmonic minor key. More on diatonic chords in Chapter 12 Tying Everything Together: Diatonic Harmony.

Be sure to follow the chord diagrams that indicate which chord form to use.

This exercise is demonstrated on Track 145.

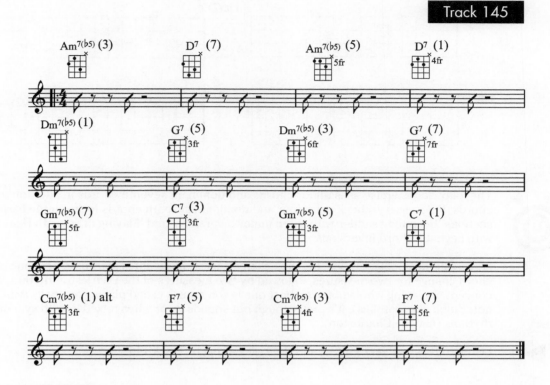

Higher strings

The following figure shows four primary inversions and one alternative inversion for the Am7♭5 chord, using only the d-, a-, and e-strings. Notice that I put numbers 1, 3, 5, and 7 next to the chord symbols to indicate the highest chord tone.

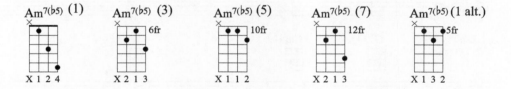

The neck diagrams in the following figure demonstrate the four most common m7♭5 chords. Each neck diagram shows the one (root), three, five, and seven forms of each chord while staying on the d-, a-, and e-strings. I show the forms with 1, 3, 5, or 7 in the white circular fret indicators. Practice all four forms of each chord until you can play them from memory, before proceeding to the next chord.

Am7♭5

Dm7♭5

Gm7♭5

Cm7♭5

The following exercise uses minor chords and dominant seventh chords in addition to m7♭5 chords. If necessary, check out minor and dominant seventh chords forms in the earlier sections 'Becoming sadder with three minor inversions' and 'Playing in Seventh Heaven with Seventh Chord Inversions'.

Staying in the cool jazz mode, the next exercise uses whole notes placed on beat one of each chord change for two measures, followed by two measures of the Charleston rhythm. The concept of playing whole notes on beat one is sometimes called playing footballs (whole notes look like footballs). It's pretty tough but sounds great when mixed in with syncopated rhythms (like the Charleston).

Listen to this cool jazz groove and then play along to Track 146.

Track 146

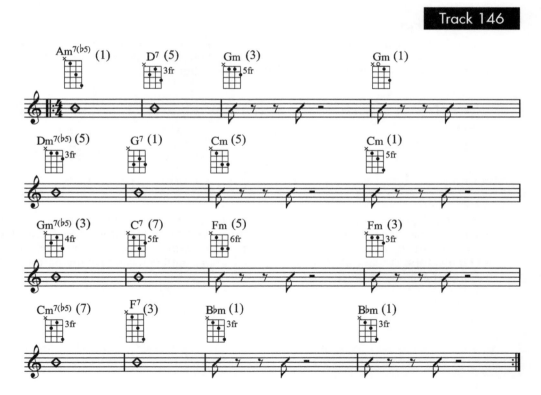

Increasing Returns with Diminished Seventh and Augmented Chords

Diminished seventh and augmented chords are based on stacking intervals in a mathematical way as opposed to having the chord tones originating in a scale (I cover this subject in Chapter 11). When playing these chords as three-string chords you use geometric shapes that are similar to those that you employ with diminished seventh and augmented arpeggios.

Securing the services of diminished seventh chords

I explain diminished seventh (dim7) chords in Chapter 11, where you discover that any of the notes in this diminished chord form can be considered the root (or name) of the chord. Notice that in the following figure, as long as the chord contains an A note, this chord is called Adim7. In fact, because you're only playing three notes of this four-note chord, form 5 of this chord doesn't even have the A note, but does contain C, E♭, and F♯. Don't forget to look over the diminished seventh chord tone table in Chapter 11.

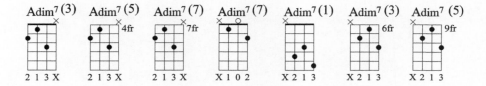

Adding augmented chords to your armory

Augmented chords are similar to the diminished seventh chords of the preceding section in that you need to know only one moveable chord form, keeping in mind that any of the notes can be the root. See the following figure for the A augmented chord forms, which can also be called C♯ augmented or F augmented. (Check out Chapter 11 for more details.)

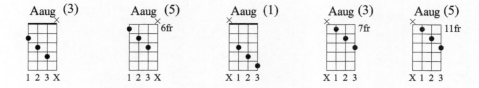

Chapter 14

Personalizing Your Playing: Improvisation

In This Chapter

▶ Taking a brief look at improvising on chord changes

▶ Applying improvisation to four musical styles

*I*mprovisation is a crucial part of musical styles such as jazz, blues, rock, and country. By acquiring skills in this area you can improve your enjoyment of mandolin playing immensely. Improvising on a tune while playing by yourself is satisfying enough, but the thrill of being part of a group of like-minded improvising musicians who're hitting their stride is unsurpassed.

This chapter applies your knowledge of chords, scales, and arpeggios to some common chord progressions in order to help unlock some of the mystery of improvisation. I present demonstrations of different styles with backing tracks so that you can practice your own improvisational ideas.

Trying Out Some Chord Progressions

Playing through the changes is jazz speak for being able to create *lines:* melodies that fit an existing set of chords. The experienced improviser can easily identify common chord progressions used in a variety of styles of music, while being able to create melodies on the spot that sound great over the chord progression. When creating melodies to fit a chord progression, whether improvised or composed, you need to have a good handle on chords, arpeggios, scales, and the style you're playing in.

The four exercises that I describe in this chapter are based on common chord progressions and styles that you need to know if you're to become a great improvising or composing mandolin player.

When soloing or playing over the changes, you must know the chord changes! Memorizing them is best, but sometimes you need to read the chord symbols. The exercises in this chapter contain chord symbols placed above the notation.

Practice the exercises in this chapter as follows:

1. **Play the demonstration track, listening carefully to the chord changes and following along with the chord symbols located above the notation.**

2. **Learn to play the solo, trying to understand the arpeggios, scales, rhythmic characteristics, and so on.**

3. **Experiment at improvising over the rhythm section, using scales, arpeggios, and even some chromatic passages (see the chapters in Parts II and III of this book).**

Exploring improvisation

Improvisation is a deep subject that many musicians study and practice for many years. One form of improvisation is the theme-and-variation type, in which the original melody is used as a starting point and the improviser tries to play the melody in a variety of ways, making subtle or not so subtle changes or variations to the original melody. Another form of improvisation is based on the chord progression of the song instead of the melody (this is called playing through the changes). In this form of improvisation, the musician attempts to create a new melody that fits the chords and may have no resemblance to the original melody at all. Musicians that spend many years honing their improvisation skills can blend both methods seamlessly.

The great jazz trumpeter Clark Terry believes that improvisation is a three-step process:

1. **Imitation:** Listening, learning licks and solos by ear from recordings, and transcribing solos.

2. **Assimilation:** Practicing and studying these licks, nuances, solos, and rhythmic and harmonic devices until they're part of your style.

3. **Innovation:** Creating a fresh approach to the music. Innovation happens only after many hours of imitation and assimilation, and is where you add your own personality.

If improvisation is your thing, you need to learn all your scales and arpeggios, but also listen very carefully to your favorite musicians and imitate them. You end up sounding a bit like your heroes, which isn't a bad thing. Eventually your own musical identity is revealed — a combination of *chops* (musical skills), taste or influences, and your own personality.

Try to play what you hear in your head – and remember: don't give up! If you want to read more about the fascinating art of improvisation, check out the nearby sidebar 'Exploring improvisation'.

Improvising in Different Genres

The type and amount of improvisation varies according to the conventions of different musical styles. In jazz, extensive improvisation on the chords is central, and the inventiveness and originality of the improvisation is often how jazz musicians are judged by their peers (and history!). For styles such as blues and country, the improvisation tends to be more melody based and less complex, but no less skilled and exciting.

In this section you get the chance to try your hand (and fingers) at four improvisation exercises.

Going where the grass grows blue: Bluegrass-style tune

Since the 1940s, one of the most common musical styles to feature mandolin is bluegrass. In fact, most people associate mandolin with bluegrass, even though your favorite instrument has a long, colorful past, including in classical music, Italian folk music, Brazilian choro music, and many other forms.

Bluegrass mandolin is a blend of fiddle tunes, which originated in the British Isles, and blues, which includes rags and even early forms of jazz from the deep south of America. This blend was invented and popularized by Bill Monroe, who's credited as the father of bluegrass music.

The following bluegrass-style exercise is in the key of B major, which is popular in bluegrass because it places the voice at the top of the singer's range, creating that characteristic high, lonesome sound. This solo consists of primarily *double stops,* or two notes of an arpeggio played at the same time, while including some of the rhythm patterns that Bill Monroe used. These patterns are shown in *Mandolin For Dummies* in Chapter 10.

So that you can better visualize the double stops as being part of the arpeggio, I include brackets under the tablature (tab), indicating which arpeggio pattern the double stop is part of. If you need to brush up on your arpeggio patterns, visit Chapters 7–10.

Pay close attention to the slides, because some require you to slide both notes of the double stop, and some require sliding only one finger while holding the other finger in place.

You can hear this example and try your luck at jamming in B major on Track 147 at www.dummies.com/go/mandolinexercises.

Track 147

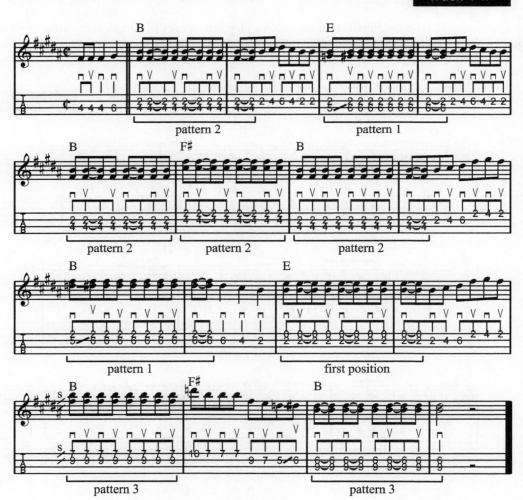

Heading to the country: I/IV/V country-style tune

This tune is based on the I/IV/V (one/four/five) chord progression used in country, blues, and folk music. The roman numerals indicate which diatonic chords are used (see the diatonic triads in major keys chord table in Chapter 12). This example is in the good old key of G major and takes full advantage of the major pentatonic and Americana scales I describe in Chapter 5.

Notice how the so-called Americana scale is used like an arpeggio, in that the scale changes for each chord. For example, during the G chord the G Americana scale is used, but when the chords change to C the C Americana scale is used, and when the D chord is used the D Americana scale is used. So even though this is a simple progression in the key of G major, in which you could just play notes from the G major scale, this approach gives the melody or solo much more color with a slight bluesy effect.

This improvised solo is played completely in open position, and you need to use alternate picking. Other techniques required for this exercise are slides, chromatic passages, and major pentatonic and Americana scales. Pay attention to the finger numbers placed above the tab.

Listen to the demonstration on Track 148, learn to play it, and then try your hand at improvising through a simple country progression using the major pentatonic and Americana scales.

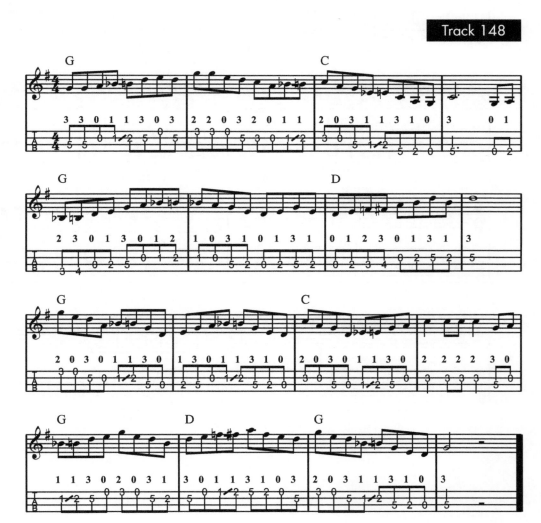

Feeling blue: Jazzy 12-bar blues

The 12-bar blues is a staple chord progression for the improvising musician. In its basic form, the 12-bar blues contains three chords. Jazz musicians tend to add some fancy chords, making the harmony more complex than you'd find in, say, delta blues or rock blues.

Another difference between traditional or delta blues is that jazz players tend to play in flat keys or keys that contain flats in the key signature. This is most likely due to the fact that saxophones and other woodwind instruments commonly used in jazz are easier to play in the keys of B♭, E♭, and even A♭. String players (that's you!) who are interested in playing jazz need to learn to play in these flat keys. The following jazzy 12-bar blues is in the key of B♭.

This tune uses a few jazzy chords and turnarounds that you should be familiar with. Here's a list of jazz changes used in the jazzy 12-bar blues:

- ✔ **Quick to the IV:** Changing to the IV chord on the second measure, then back to the I chord on the third measure, instead of playing four bars of the I chord.

- ✔ **Diminished walk up:** Playing a diminished chord, one half step higher than the IV chord, following the IV chord in measure five. You play the diminished chord in measure six.

- ✔ **VI7/II7/V7/I:** Pronounced 'six-two-five-one', this is a common turnaround. In the key of B♭ the chords are G7/C7/F7/B♭. By looking at the chord symbols placed above the notation you can see this turnaround beginning at measure eight.

Play this improvised melody completely in open position, using all down-strokes. Other techniques used are slides, triplets, and swing eighth notes, which I cover in *Mandolin For Dummies,* along with arpeggios and chromatic passages (see Part III and Chapter 5 of this book, respectively). You may want to review these techniques if you're unsure about how to perform them.

Watch out for the *accidentals* (sharps and flats). The proper left hand fingerings are shown directly above the tab.

Listen to this jazzy 12-bar blues in B♭ on Track 149.

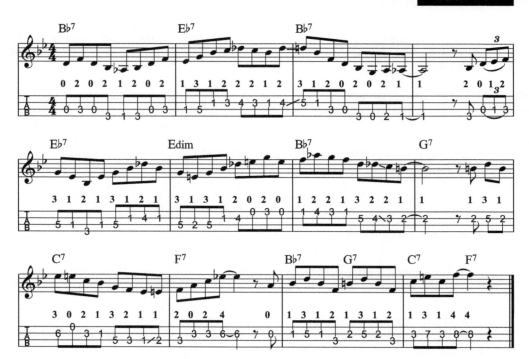

Playing over the moon: 32-bar jazz standard

Jazz is a bit of a mystery and can be intimidating to musicians because of the sheer number of complex chords in any one song. Practicing how to see groups of chords and organize them by key is crucial to understanding harmonically what's going on in this music.

Jazz is a pretty deep well, but Chapter 13 of *Mandolin For Dummies* explains much of what a budding jazz mandolin player needs to know in order to start playing some jazzy-style tunes.

The following exercise borrows a chord progression from a famous jazz standard *How High The Moon*. The great jazz saxophone player Charlie Parker used this very same chord progression for his classic bebop tune 'Ornithology'. Play this track at a fairly slow tempo using all down-strokes.

This tune starts in the key of G major but quickly moves to the key of F major. The key changes at the Gm7 chord, with the Gm7 being the ii chord and the C7 being the V7 chord in the key of F major. See the diatonic seventh chord table in Chapter 12 'Playing Diatonic Triads in Major Keys'.

This progression is called a ii/V7/I (or 'two-five-one'). Notice this same progression of Fm7/B♭7 leading to the key of E♭, followed by Am7♭5/D7 leading to the key of Gm. You need to be able to spot these ii/V7/I progressions if you plan on playing much jazz.

Play the first 16 bars in the following figure in open position; the second 16 bars use some up-the-neck positions. Follow the fingerings that are shown directly above the tab.

I demonstrate this 32-bar jazz standard chord progression on Track 150.

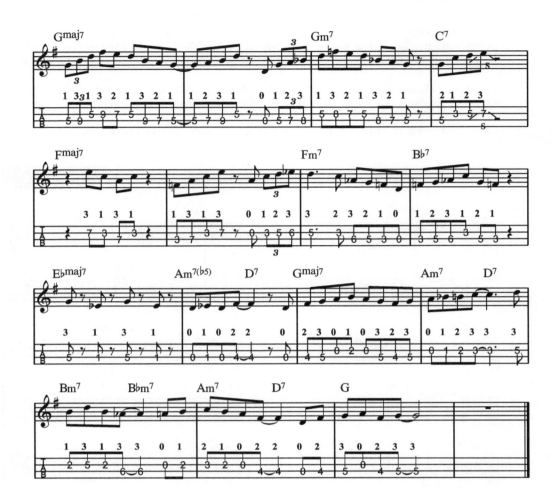

Part V
The Part of Tens

Go to www.dummies.com/go/mandolinexercises for free downloadable audio content.

In this part . . .

✔ Practise, learn and play ten tunes using everything you've learned from this book.

✔ Become a mandolin master and increase your playing speed while maintaining a clean, clear sound.

Chapter 15

Ten Top Tunes to Put Your Skills to Good Use

In This Chapter
▶ Applying scales and scale patterns to great tunes
▶ Spotting arpeggios in pieces of music

*E*xercises are, of course, only a means to an end: playing any instrument is all about performing complete pieces of music and seeing the impressed look on your friends' faces. So in this chapter I present ten tunes for you to learn that incorporate many of the scales, chords, and arpeggios you've been practicing.

I arrange these tunes in no particular order. You will find a lullaby, a couple of fiddle tunes, 2 simple classical style pieces, some jazz, some blues, a bit of gypsy, and a couple of film score style tunes, all written for the mandolin. I suggest you browse through all ten and learn the ones that you like.

Be sure to download all the tracks that go with *Mandolin Exercises For Dummies* at www.dummies.com/go/mandolinexercises. Listen to each tune a few times before trying to play it. Have fun! And play that mandolin!

'Goodnight'

This tune is a simple little lullaby in the key of G major. Notice that the three-string triads in measures 5–11 are played on the d-, a-, and e-strings, while the g-string rings out through all the chords. This effect is called a *drone* or a *pedal tone*.

Play this piece very gently with expression. You can hear it on Track 151.

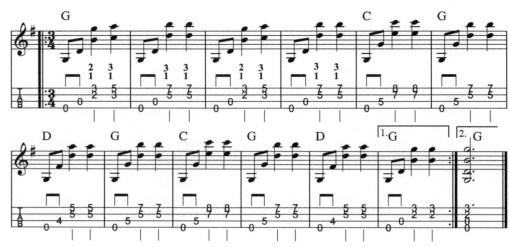

Reproduced by the permission of Don Julin

'The String Changing Tune'

This is a simple two-part fiddle tune in A major and uses drone strings and alternate picking. Remember that fiddle tunes are played in the form AABB (see *Mandolin For Dummies* Chapter 9). Notice the use of the blue note (see Chapter 5) (C) sliding into the C♯ in the A part.

Listen to this piece on Track 152 and have fun with 'The String Changing Tune'. You don't have to reserve it only for when a musical partner breaks a string!

Track 152

Reproduced by the permission of Don Julin

'Munchkin Dance'

'Munchkin Dance' is a pseudo-classical light-hearted dance in C major, played completely in open position. This tune uses nothing more than the C major scale and the C, F, G, and G7 arpeggios. Use alternate picking for the eighth notes (quavers) and down-stokes for the quarter notes (crotchets). Pay attention to the staccato marks (dots) placed above or below the notation and tablature indicating to shorten the note leaving a small amount of silence between the notes that have the staccato markings.

I demonstrate 'Munchkin Dance' on Track 153.

Reproduced by the permission of Don Julin

'Diminishing Returns'

'Diminishing Returns' is a swinging 1930s style jazz tune based on a series of arpeggios, including major, minor seventh, dominant seventh, and diminished types. This piece, in the key of G major, remains in open position; you should play it using either alternate picking or all down-stokes, depending on the tempo you choose.

Listen to 'Diminishing Returns' on Track 154.

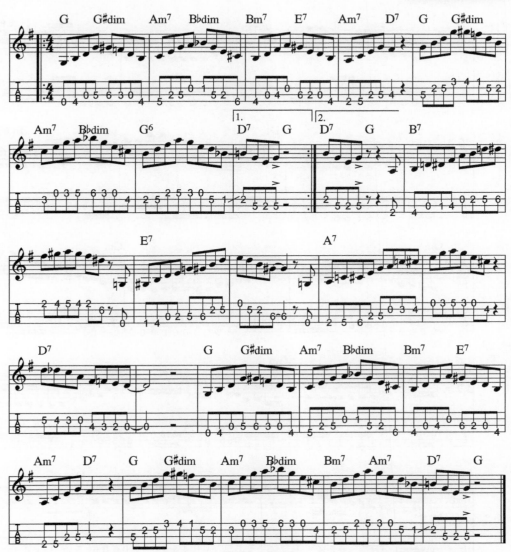

Reproduced by the permission of Don Julin

'You Say Etude, I Say Atude'

'You Say Etude, I Say Atude' is in G minor, using two-octave arpeggios (see Chapters 7 and 8). The G minor arpeggio uses open position for the lower octave and pattern 1 (from Chapter 8) for the higher octave. C minor arpeggios use pattern 2 (also from Chapter 8) and pattern 1. The D arpeggio uses open position and pattern 1 at the fifth fret (see Chapter 7). The A7 arpeggio lower octave uses pattern 1, with the higher one being open (see Chapter 9).

Listen to 'You Say Etude, I Say Atude' on Track 155.

Reproduced by the permission of Don Julin

'Fellini'

'Fellini' is a waltz inspired by the Italian film maker Federico Fellini, in E minor, which uses the E harmonic minor scale, (Chapter 4) tremolo, (*Mandolin For Dummies*) a descending chromatic theme, (Chapter 5) and the B augmented arpeggios (see Chapter 11).

This piece begins with a harmonic minor scale with a long first-finger slide from the second fret to the sixth fret of the a-string. This slide not only sounds quite dramatic, but also gets you in position to play the descending theme with tremolo. Notice that you play the main theme (measures 1–5) on one string.

You can find scale and arpeggio one-string patterns and exercises in Chapters 3-5 and 7-11. This type of melody is an example of where playing on one string can yield a lovely lyrical sound.

Listen to 'Fellini' (the tune, not the man!) on Track 156.

Track 156

Reproduced by the permission of Don Julin

'Black Squirrel'

'Black Squirrel' is a fiddle tune in two different keys, but don't panic. The A part is in the key of A major, while the B part is in the key of Am, starting on the Dm, which is the iv chord in the key of Am.

Notice that in this tune the key signature is used to indicate the key change. Being a fiddle tune, 'Black Squirrel' is best played using alternate picking. This tune also has a third part, commonly called a *tag*, used only at the very end of the song.

You can hear 'Black Squirrel' on Track 157.

Reproduced by the permission of Don Julin

'One Riff'

As its title implies, 'One Riff' is a 12-bar blues based on one single *riff* (a melodic phrase). This riff is based on the pattern 3 dominant seventh chord pattern shown in Chapter 9. Although it contains a *passing* tone (a tone that's not part of the arpeggio) and a grace note slide, (see *Mandolin For Dummies* for more on slide techniques). I think you'll be able to see how this riff is based on pattern 3.

As the chords change, the same pattern is simply moved to another location on the fingerboard to match the chord progression. Also, notice how the phrase is anticipated – that is, placed slightly before the actual chord change.

I play 'One Riff' for you on Track 158; use all down-strokes.

Reproduced by the permission of Don Julin

'Bela'

'Bela' is a waltz in the style of an eastern European folk song in the key of A minor, using the harmonic minor scale (see Chapter 4) for the entire piece. This tune is inspired by two Bela's: the actor Bela Lugosi (Dracula), and the modern classical composer Bela Bartok. Take note of the E7 arpeggios in the second part. Use standard alternate picking, making the eighth notes (quavers) alternate and the quarter notes (crotchets) all down-strokes.

You can hear 'Bela' on Track 159.

Track 159

Reproduced by the permission of Don Julin

'Jig, Not A Jig'

'Jig, Not A Jig' is in 6/8 time and uses the standard jig-picking pattern of down-up-down-down-up-down per measure. Mind you, that's about the only thing about this tune that resembles an Irish jig. It actually sounds more like a science fiction film score than an Irish jig.

Harmonically this piece is in three keys using the same theme for each of the three keys. It starts in the key of F major and is played out of major scale pattern 1 (see Chapter 3). Next it moves to the key of G major and is also played out of major scale pattern 1 by simply moving your left hand up two frets and playing the same thing you played in the key of F.

The next key change goes up another whole step to the key of A major, but this time instead of just moving your left hand up two more frets, you move your left hand to the end of the neck and play the same theme in open position in the key of A major. I suggest playing through the entire piece at least twice.

Listen to 'Jig, Not a Jig' on Track 160.

Reproduced by the permission of Don Julin

Chapter 16

Ten Tempting Tips on Tempo to Increase Your Playing Speed

In This Chapter

▶ Getting your hands ready to play quickly

▶ Using a metronome to help you improve

▶ Making sure your mandolin is capable of going fast

Speed isn't everything, of course, although escaping criminals may disagree. But the mandolin is well set up as an instrument for speed, and playing quickly is great fun. Yet to the novice mandolin player, speed can appear extremely intimidating. (Some players even claim that they don't want to play quickly, although I don't believe them.) Fiddle tunes, tremolo, bluegrass, and most mandolin styles require an agile and quick right hand.

The ten tips that I present in this chapter increase your mandolin speed and your playing confidence. So, to discover how to burn mandolin rubber (so to speak), read on.

Making Best Use of Your Metronome

Metronomes are a great practice tool, and like with most tools you need to find out how to use them properly. Although you can buy plenty of fancy metronomes that subdivide beats and play different pitches for each beat, I still prefer an electronic metronome with a loud, sharp click, not a beep. The first thing that you notice about playing with a metronome is that it doesn't follow you; you need to follow it. As a result, you have to listen to the beat and relax. If you're nervous, you speed up. Everyone does.

The goal is to play steadily without speeding up at the easy parts and slowing down at the hard parts. When you can play steadily, you're ready to start turning up the tempo.

Using Proper Right-Hand Technique

The right hand is the one that strikes the strings, and so you need to pay extra attention to pick grip, pick shape, pick thickness and even pick material, in order to play in a relaxed style at faster tempos.

Although you find variations in technique among top pro players, all good mandolin players agree that you need a good understanding of alternate picking. (If you need a review, go to *Mandolin For Dummies,* Chapter 5.) In its simplest form, alternate picking is a repeating down-up-down-up pick stroke. You can do this on one string or more, on one single note, or on a complete run or melody. By practicing alternate-picking exercises such as the ones in Chapter 2, you gain more control and confidence with your right hand, resulting in the ability to play more smoothly and quickly.

Hearing the Melody at Target Tempo

A wise musician once said, 'If you can't say it, you can't play it.'

Practice singing the melodies that you want to play quickly. Start slowly and get the notes right, gradually picking up speed.

You should be able to sing all the fiddle tunes that you can play, and even the ones you want to play but haven't mastered yet. You can never play anything on the mandolin faster than you can say or sing it.

Loosening Your Pick Grip

A death grip on the pick is a sure way never to reach your goal of playing fast and smoothly. Mandolin players tend to use a fairly stiff pick with a very loose grip – the latter tying in with the idea of staying relaxed, because you can't play in a relaxed way with a death grip.

Tremolo, being nothing more than very fast alternate picking, also requires a very loose grip on the pick.

Practicing Slowly to Pick Up Speed

You may not believe me until you try this tip, but playing slowly can help you increase speed. I'm talking about playing very slowly: perhaps 50 per cent or even less of the target tempo. As you play faster, your technique becomes more important. This advice applies to pick direction for the right hand and proper fingerings and articulations for the left hand.

As tempos increase, you'll certainly run across some trouble areas that are difficult to play cleanly, but continuing to practice them quickly will only ensure that they remain problematic, making the situation worse. The old saying 'practice makes perfect' is more accurately stated as 'practice makes permanent'. So practicing a song but messing up the really tough part every time doesn't only sound less than perfect, but can and will make it harder for you to correct problems in the long run.

Slowing down to half speed or even slower requires you to pay attention to the beginning, middle, and end of each note, along with which finger plays the note and the direction in which the pick is moving in order to play the note. In other words, you can't just skim over the tough parts when you play very slowly. When you've fixed the tough parts and can play them slowly with proper technique, you're then able to increase the speed.

Don't be fooled into thinking that you can play a tune quickly but for some reason you just can't play it slowly!

Discovering Some Metronome Tricks

Owning a metronome is a good thing, using it when you practice is better, and understanding this basic metronome exercise is better still. When first using a metronome, most people set the click to match the quarter note (quaver); so in 4/4 time you hear four clicks, one for each beat.

Assume that you're working on a fiddle tune at the speed of 160 beats per minute (bpm) in 4/4 time with many eighth notes (crotchets), and follow these steps:

1. **Set the metronome to 160 (or whatever speed you can comfortably play the tune) so that the click is on every other note (or all the down-beats) and play the tune.** Easy enough.

2. **Cut the metronome speed in half to 80 bpm, so that it clicks on beats one and three only.** The music is the same tempo, but the click is on every other quarter note. Now you're responsible for keeping four eighth notes steady between each click of the metronome. Practice the tune with the metronome on beats one and three.

3. **Leave the metronome set at 80 bpm, but now have the clicks on beats two and four instead of one and three.** Yes, your metronome can do this, and no special settings are needed. Just a simple metronome set to 80 bpm. By practicing with a metronome on the backbeat, your timing improves dramatically. Trust me: this really works!

The following figure illustrates the three methods: (a) set at 160 bpm on all four beats; (b) set to 80 bpm on beats one and three; and (c) set to 80 bpm on beats two and four. The 'x's indicate where the metronome click lands.

`Track 161`

(a) 1+2+3+4+ 1+2+3+4+ (b) 1+2+3+4+ 1+2+3+4+ (c) 1+2+3+4+ 1+2+3+4+

On Track 161 you can hear a demonstration of the type of metronome practice technique. Visit www.dummies.com/go/mandolinexercises for all the book's accompanying downloadable tracks.

Playing Along with Recordings

Playing along with recordings is a great way to get comfortable with the tempos and techniques needed for the style of music you want to play. If you're a blues lover, play along with your favorite blues artists whether they are mandolin players or not, the blues feel is what is important; if Brazilian choro is more your thing, try performing with some choro recordings. Jacob do Bandolim is considered the greatest of all Brazilian choro mandolin players.

After spending some time on this, you may find that recordings that once seemed to be played incredibly quickly turn out to be within your reach. This approach ties in to the concept of 'if you can't say it, you can't play it' (see the earlier section 'Hearing the Melody at Target Tempo'), but adds the physicality of trying to keep up. If the melodies are just too fast at first, practice an appropriate rhythm pattern for the style of music, and play along with the rhythm section by chording and strumming at the real tempo, playing with your real musical heroes.

Setting up Your Instrument's Action

The term *action* on a mandolin refers to the distance by which you need to depress the strings until they sit firmly on a fret. In order to have low, easy-to-play action, your mandolin needs to be set up correctly. When the action is low it is easier to fret the notes making it easier to play fast.

Consider taking your mandolin to a qualified luthier to assess the straightness of the neck, make sure that the frets aren't worn down, that they're crowned properly, and that the nut slots cut the right depth. When your mandolin is set up properly, you're able to adjust the action and get it so that you need very little left-hand pressure to fret notes cleanly.

Just because people are good at working on guitars doesn't automatically make them good on mandolins. The fact that the mandolin neck is shorter and the strings are strung very tightly and in pairs means that getting the action low but not buzzing is very important. Make the extra effort to locate a mandolin expert when your mandolin needs a set-up or an action adjustment.

Most pro mandolin players have their action set somewhere in the range of 0.010–0.015 inches (0.254–0.381 millimeters) at the nut. This measurement is the distance by which you need to press the open string until it frets cleanly at the first fret. The other place commonly measured is at the 12th fret, which is normally set at 0.05–0.07 inches (1.27–1.778 millimeters), depending on the player's preference. Higher action can result in more volume but makes the mandolin physically harder to play.

Staying Relaxed

Take a full breath and slowly let it out; repeat this process a few times. Can you hear your heartbeat? It shouldn't be racing, but steady and slow. Playing mandolin can be a source of great anxiety, especially when trying to keep up with a fast tune.

The best advice I ever heard regarding this situation is 'keep breathing'. I know that seems silly to even mention, but pay attention the next time you get a little tense or have trouble playing something as fast as you think you should, and I bet you're also holding your breath. If you're not breathing correctly, your brain isn't getting the proper amount of oxygen. If your brain is starved of oxygen . . . well you know where this is going.

Just remember to breathe at a steady pace, and you're half way to relaxation. You need to be very relaxed to play quickly without sounding forced or choppy, and so take a deep breath in, exhale, and play mandolin.

Never think that you need to play at your very top speed. This is a very bad mental state to be in and about as far from relaxed as you can possibly get. The only solution to thinking that you can't play very quickly is to discover how to play fast: even faster than your target is best.

Increasing by Small Increments

What if you follow all the steps in this chapter and can play the desired tune slowly, with a metronome, using proper fingerings and correct pick direction, but you still can't seem to play very quickly? Follow the easy steps I provide in this section and you'll be playing the tune up to speed in no time.

Imagine that your work in progress is an Irish reel and the target tempo is a blurring 114 bpm with two metronome clicks per measure. The best you can do is about 80 bpm before you crash and burn:

1. **Play the tune using proper left-hand fingerings and correct pick direction at 60 bpm or any speed that you're sure you can play cleanly.** Play the tune with your metronome at least six times through from beginning to end. If you find yourself making mistakes, you may need to isolate the mistakes and fix them before you go on.

2. **Increase the metronome by 4 or 6 bpm.** Play through the tune at least six times without mistakes. Stay at this tempo until you can achieve this feat.

3. **Continue increasing the tempo by 4 or 6 bpm.** Make sure that you're playing mistake-free for at least six times before moving on.

4. **Make a note of the metronome marking when you reach your top mistake-free speed.** But this time, keep going even if you make a few mistakes until you can't go any faster without total disaster.

5. **Go back to the tempo you marked as your top speed in step 4.** You'll be surprised how easy playing at this tempo is, allowing you to enjoy playing the tune without any anxiety about not being able to play quickly. Repeat this exercise daily!

Appendix

Using the Audio Tracks

● ●

To help you get the most out of *Mandolin Exercises For Dummies*, I've recorded hundreds of audio tracks to help you with the exercises and songs you can find in this book. This allows you to listen and play along; giving you a much better idea of how the exercise or song should sound as you practice it.

Using the Audio Tracks with this Book

Exercises or songs that have a corresponding audio track are indicated with a black box above the figure, which tells you the track number.

Downloading the audio tracks

To listen to the *Mandolin Exercises For Dummies* audio tracks, visit the following website address to download and open the audio tracks on your computer:

www.dummies.com/go/mandolinexercises

Master List of Audio Tracks

The following is a complete list of the audio tracks that accompany this book. Download the audio tracks from www.dummies.com/go/mandolinexercises.

Track	Description
1	Tuning
2	Alternate picking review
3	Tremolo Exercise
4	String Skipping Exercise
5	Tetrachords
6	Major scale pattern 1
7	Major scale pattern 1 seq
8	Major scale pattern 2
9	Major scale pattern 2 seq
10	Major scale pattern 3
11	Major scale pattern 3 seq
12	Major scale pattern 4
13	Major scale pattern 4 seq
14	Major scales exercise
15	Natural minor scale pattern 1
16	Natural minor scale pattern 1 seq
17	Natural minor scale pattern 2
18	Natural minor scale pattern 2 seq
19	Natural minor scale pattern 3
20	Natural minor scale pattern 3 seq
21	Natural minor scale pattern 4
22	Natural minor scale pattern 4 seq
23	Natural minor scales exercise
24	Harmonic Minor scale pattern 1
25	Harmonic Minor scale pattern 1 seq
26	Harmonic Minor scale pattern 2
27	Harmonic Minor scale pattern 2 seq
28	Harmonic Minor scale pattern 3
29	Harmonic Minor scale pattern 3 seq
30	Harmonic Minor scale pattern 4
31	Harmonic Minor scale pattern 4 seq
32	Harmonic Minor scales exercise
33	Melodic Minor scale pattern 1
34	Melodic Minor scale pattern 1 seq
35	Melodic Minor scale pattern 2
36	Melodic Minor scale pattern 2 seq
37	Melodic Minor scale pattern 3
38	Melodic Minor scale pattern 3 seq
39	Melodic Minor scale pattern 4
40	Melodic Minor scale pattern 4 seq
41	Melodic Minor scales exercise
42	Major Pentatonic scale pattern 1

Track	*Description*
43	Major Pentatonic pattern 1 lick
44	Major Pentatonic scale pattern 2
45	Major Pentatonic pattern 2 lick
46	Major Pentatonic scale pattern 3
47	Major Pentatonic pattern 3 lick
48	Major Pentatonic scale pattern 4
49	Major Pentatonic pattern 4 lick
50	'Flatt' run
51	'Flatt' run in 6 keys
52	G, C, D, solo
53	D, G, A, solo
54	Minor Pentatonic scale pattern 1
55	Minor Pentatonic scale pattern 2
56	Minor Pentatonic scale pattern 3
57	Minor Pentatonic scale pattern 4
58	Chromatic fingering
59	Blues lick in 6 keys
60	12 bar blues in G
61	Chromatic one fret
62	Chromatic two frets
63	Crucial scale sequences
64	Pattern 1-4 seq
65	Pattern 2-1 seq
66	Entire fingerboard
67	Pattern 3-2 seq
68	Apply to all scales
69	Pattern 4-3 seq
70	Shift six ways
71	One finger shift
72	All finger shift
73	Two finger shift
74	7th fret shift
75	Major arpeggios pattern 1
76	Major arpeggios pattern 2
77	Major arpeggios pattern 3
78	Major arpeggios pattern 4
79	Major arpeggios in 6 keys exercise
80	One string minor arpeggio exercise
81	2 octave major arpeggio exercise
82	Minor arpeggio pattern 1
83	Minor arpeggio pattern 2
84	Minor arpeggio pattern 3
85	Minor arpeggio pattern 4
86	Minor arpeggios in 6 keys exercise
87	One string minor arpeggio exercise
88	2 octave minor arpeggio exercise
89	Major 7th arpeggios pattern 1

Track	*Description*
90	Major 7th arpeggios pattern 2
91	Major 7th arpeggios pattern 3
92	Major 7th arpeggios pattern 4
93	Major 7th moveable arpeggio exercise
94	Maj7 first position arpeggio exercise
95	2 octave major 7th arpeggio patterns
96	7th arpeggios pattern 1
97	7th arpeggios pattern 2
98	7th arpeggios pattern 3
99	7th arpeggios pattern 4
100	7th moveable arpeggios exercise
101	7th first position arpeggios exercise
102	2 octave 7th arpeggio patterns
103	Minor 7th arpeggios pattern 1
104	Minor 7th arpeggios pattern 2
105	Minor 7th arpeggios pattern 3
106	Minor 7th arpeggios pattern 4
107	Minor 7th moveable arpeggio exercise
108	Minor 7th first position arpeggio exercise
109	2 octave minor 7th arpeggio patterns
110	Minor 7♭5 arpeggios pattern 1
111	Minor 7♭5 arpeggios pattern 2
112	Minor 7♭5 arpeggios pattern 3
113	Minor 7♭5 arpeggios pattern 4
114	Minor 7♭5 moveable arpeggios exercise
115	Minor 7♭5 first position arpeggio exercise
116	2 octave minor 7♭5 arpeggio patterns
117	Diminished diagonal pattern
118	Diminished cascading exercise
119	Dim7 first position ex
120	Aug diagonal pattern
121	Aug diagonal pattern exercise
122	Aug first position exercise
123	Major key Diatonic triads 1-4
124	Major key Diatonic triads 2-1
125	Major key Diatonic triads 3-2
126	Major key Diatonic triads 4-3
127	Major key Diatonic 7ths 1-4
128	Major key Diatonic 7ths 2-1
129	Major key Diatonic 7ths 3-2
130	Major key Diatonic 7ths 4-3
131	Minor key Diatonic triads 1-4
132	Minor key Diatonic triads 2-1
133	Minor key Diatonic triads 3-2
134	Minor key Diatonic triads 4-3
135	Major chord exercise lo
136	Major chord exercise hi

Track	*Description*
137	Minor chord exercise lo
138	Minor chord exercise hi
139	Maj7 chord exercise lo
140	Maj7 chord exercise hi
141	7th chord exercise lo
142	7th chord exercise hi
143	M7 chord exercise lo
144	M7 chord exercise hi
145	M7♭5 chord exercise lo
146	M7♭5 chord exercise hi
147	Bluegrass style solo
148	I/IV/V country style
149	Jazzy 12 bar blues
150	32 bar standard
151	'Goodnight'
152	'The string changing tune'
153	'Munchkin Dance'
154	'Diminishing returns'
155	'You Say Etude, I Say Atude'
156	'Fellini'
157	'Black Squirrel'
158	'One Riff'
159	'Bela'
160	'Jig, Not A Jig'
161	Metronome tricks

Index

....

● *N* ●

Notes

Notes

Notes

About the Author

Don Julin has worn many hats during his 30 plus years in the music business, including educator, performer, composer, arranger, conductor, recording engineer, record producer and author; but above all he is a mandolin player.

Don is currently touring with the duo *Billy Strings & Don Julin* http://donjulin.com/billystrings.html playing old school bluegrass with an extreme attitude. Keep an eye out for them as they may be in your town soon. When not playing with Billy Strings, Don can be seen in northern Michigan playing with a variety of groups including *The Neptune Quartet*, jazz guitarist Ron Getz, or just playing solo mandolin in a corner of a nice restaurant.

As a mandolin teacher Don offers private instruction via Skype or in person, having held mandolin workshops and master classes around the world including *Elderly Instruments* in Lansing, Michigan, *Ceasar Pollini Conservatory of Music* in Padova, Italy and Davig Grisman and Mike Marshall's *Mandolin Symposium* in Santa Cruz, California. He has many free mini-lessons posted on YouTube www.youtube.com/donjulinlessons and is available for workshops or master classes. Don currently lives in Traverse City, Michigan.

Don has released 13 CDs of original music and played on countless others. His original compositions have been used on many network and cable television programs along with NPR's *All things Considered*. Recent clients include HBO, VH1, MTV, NBC, Showtime, Bravo, National Geographic Explorer, Fox Sports, Hermann Miller Corp. and Unitarian Universalist Association of Congregations.

For lessons, workshops, booking or to just talk about mandolins you can reach Don through his website at www.donjulin.com.

Author's Acknowledgments

As a full time musician/player for over 30 years, I consider myself to be one of the luckiest people in the world. I would like to take this time to thank many of the people that have helped shaped my life through encouragement, example or just by being there. Thank you all.

Scott Tichenor, Bill Monroe, David Grisman, Sam Bush, Jethro Burns, Don Steirnberg, Mike Compton, Alan Epstein, Zeke Little, Ruffo, William Apostol, Unzan Pfennig, Adam Steffey, Chris Thile, Rich DelGrosso, Marla Fibish, Andy Statman, Dave Apollon, John Abercrombie, Ron Getz, Jack Dryden, Randy Marsh, Ralph Stanley, Doc Watson, Mike Marshall, Bob Farmer, I Am Wes, Chet Janik, The Microtones, Big Swifty & Associates, The Neptune Quartet, Rusty Blaides, Dud Maia, Miles Davis, Mom, Bill Frisell, Sun Ra, Berrien Thorne, Little Bohemia, Frank Zappa, Ted McManus, John Hartford, Jacob do Bandolim, Tiny Moore, Frank Wakefield, Yank Rachell, and many more that I just can't remember right now. Thank you.

Publisher's Acknowledgments

We're proud of this book; please send us your comments at http://dummies.custhelp.com. For other comments, please contact our Customer Care Department within the U.S. at 877-762-2974, outside the U.S. at (001) 317-572-3993, or fax 317-572-4002.

Some of the people who helped bring this book to market include the following:

Acquisitions, Editorial, and Vertical Websites

Project Editor: Jo Jones

Commissioning Editor: Mike Baker

Assistant Editor: Ben Kemble

Development Editor: Andy Finch

Technical Editor: Matt Flinner

Copyeditor: Mary White

Proofreader: Melanie Assinder-Smith

Production Manager: Daniel Mersey

Publisher: Miles Kendall

Cover Photo: ©iStockphoto.com/vid64

FOR DUMMIES®

Making Everything Easier! ™

UK editions

BUSINESS

Bookkeeping For Dummies
978-1-118-34689-1

Pop Up Business For Dummies
978-1-118-44349-1

Starting & Running a Business All-in-One For Dummies
978-1-119-97527-4

MUSIC

Mandolin For Dummies
978-1-119-94276-4

Ukulele For Dummies
978-0-470-97799-6

DJing For Dummies
978-0-470-66372-1

HOBBIES

Stargazing For Dummies
978-1-118-41156-8

Keeping Chickens For Dummies
978-1-119-99417-6

Beekeeping For Dummies
978-1-119-97250-1

Asperger's Syndrome For Dummies
978-0-470-66087-4

Basic Maths For Dummies
978-1-119-97452-9

Body Language For Dummies, 2nd Edition
978-1-119-95351-7

Boosting Self-Esteem For Dummies
978-0-470-74193-1

Business Continuity For Dummies
978-1-118-32683-1

Cricket For Dummies
978-0-470-03454-5

Diabetes For Dummies, 3rd Edition
978-0-470-97711-8

eBay For Dummies, 3rd Edition
978-1-119-94122-4

English Grammar For Dummies
978-0-470-05752-0

Flirting For Dummies
978-0-470-74259-4

IBS For Dummies
978-0-470-51737-6

ITIL For Dummies
978-1-119-95013-4

Management For Dummies, 2nd Edition
978-0-470-97769-9

Managing Anxiety with CBT For Dummies
978-1-118-36606-6

Neuro-linguistic Programming For Dummies, 2nd Edition
978-0-470-66543-5

Nutrition For Dummies, 2nd Edition
978-0-470-97276-2

Organic Gardening For Dummies
978-1-119-97706-3

FOR DUMMIES®

Making Everything Easier!™

UK editions

SELF-HELP

Cognitive Behavioural Therapy For Dummies
978-0-470-66541-1

Creative Visualization For Dummies
978-1-119-99264-6

Mindfulness For Dummies
978-0-470-66086-7

LANGUAGES

Spanish For Dummies
978-0-470-68815-1

Polish For Dummies
978-1-119-97959-3

British Sign Language For Dummies
978-0-470-69477-0

HISTORY

The Tudors For Dummies
978-0-470-68792-5

Medieval History For Dummies
978-0-470-74783-4

British History For Dummies
978-0-470-97819-1

Origami Kit For Dummies
978-0-470-75857-1

Overcoming Depression For Dummies
978-0-470-69430-5

Positive Psychology For Dummies
978-0-470-72136-0

PRINCE2 For Dummies, 2009 Edition
978-0-470-71025-8

Project Management For Dummies
978-0-470-71119-4

Psychology Statistics For Dummies
978-1-119-95287-9

Psychometric Tests For Dummies
978-0-470-75366-8

Renting Out Your Property For Dummies, 3rd Edition
978-1-119-97640-0

Rugby Union For Dummies, 3rd Edition
978-1-119-99092-5

Sage One For Dummies
978-1-119-95236-7

Self-Hypnosis For Dummies
978-0-470-66073-7

Storing and Preserving Garden Produce For Dummies
978-1-119-95156-8

Teaching English as a Foreign Language For Dummies
978-0-470-74576-2

Time Management For Dummies
978-0-470-77765-7

Training Your Brain For Dummies
978-0-470-97449-0

Voice and Speaking Skills For Dummies
978-1-119-94512-3

Work-Life Balance For Dummies
978-0-470-71380-8

FOR DUMMIES®

Making Everything Easier! ™

COMPUTER BASICS

Laptops FOR DUMMIES

978-1-118-11533-6

PCs ALL-IN-ONE FOR DUMMIES

978-0-470-61454-9

Windows 7 FOR DUMMIES

978-0-470-49743-2

DIGITAL PHOTOGRAPHY

Digital Photography FOR DUMMIES

978-1-118-09203-3

Digital SLR Photography ALL-IN-ONE FOR DUMMIES

978-0-470-76878-5

Nikon D3100 FOR DUMMIES

978-1-118-00472-2

SCIENCE AND MATHS

Anatomy & Physiology FOR DUMMIES

978-0-470-92326-9

Algebra I FOR DUMMIES

978-0-470-55964-2

Physics I FOR DUMMIES

978-0-470-90324-7

Art For Dummies
978-0-7645-5104-8

Computers For Seniors For Dummies, 3rd Edition
978-1-118-11553-4

Criminology For Dummies
978-0-470-39696-4

Currency Trading For Dummies, 2nd Edition
978-0-470-01851-4

Drawing For Dummies, 2nd Edition
978-0-470-61842-4

Forensics For Dummies
978-0-7645-5580-0

French For Dummies, 2nd Edition
978-1-118-00464-7

Guitar For Dummies, 2nd Edition
978-0-7645-9904-0

Hinduism For Dummies
978-0-470-87858-3

Index Investing For Dummies
978-0-470-29406-2

Islamic Finance For Dummies
978-0-470-43069-9

Knitting For Dummies, 2nd Edition
978-0-470-28747-7

Music Theory For Dummies, 2nd Edition
978-1-118-09550-8

Office 2010 For Dummies
978-0-470-48998-7

Piano For Dummies, 2nd Edition
978-0-470-49644-2

Photoshop CS6 For Dummies
978-1-118-17457-9

Schizophrenia For Dummies
978-0-470-25927-6

WordPress For Dummies, 5th Edition
978-1-118-38318-6

Think you can't learn it in a day? Think again!

The *In a Day* e-book series from *For Dummies* gives you quick and easy access to learn a new skill, brush up on a hobby, or enhance your personal or professional life — all in a day. Easy!

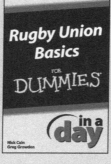